By Andrew Tully

NOVELS:

Supreme Court

Capitol Hill

A Race of Rebels

NONFICTION:

Where Did Your Money Go? (*with Milton Britten*)

Berlin: Story of a Battle

CIA: The Inside Story

When They Burned the White House

Treasury Agent

Era of Elegance

Where
Did Your Money Go?

THE FOREIGN AID STORY

Andrew Tully and Milton Britten

SIMON AND SCHUSTER : NEW YORK : 1964

The authors would like to thank Professor Hans J. Morgenthau for permission to quote from his article in the June 1962 issue of the *American Political Science Review*.

The authors are indebted beyond ability to repay to Miss Joann Sloane of the United Press-International Bureau in Washington, who did most of the research for this book.

To the American Taxpayer

Contents

The authors of this book are not opposed to foreign aid. So long as the Cold War persists, helping our friends will be just as much a part of our defense as missiles and tanks. But we are opposed to the waste and the needless foreign policy frustrations caused by the careless and sometimes corrupt administration of America's foreign aid program. This book deals with the waste and frustrations which have been the bitter fruits of the program. We hope it is a piece of constructive muckraking which, by informing the American people, will bring about needed reforms in a needed program.

—ANDREW TULLY
—MILTON BRITTEN

1 *The $40 Million Road*

"The road," said Wisconsin's liberal, Democratic Representative Henry S. Reuss, "is of little help to the Cambodians because it is unrelated to their way of life, their rice paddies and their water buffalo. On the contrary, thrust into the middle of that way of life, the road is an inevitable target for the kind of deterioration that has taken place."

Representative Reuss, a member of the House Foreign Operations Subcommittee, was talking about one place American foreign aid money went—or, more accurately, went astray. It went into 132 miles of road linking the Cambodian capital of Phnom Penh with the port of Sihanoukville on the Gulf of Siam.

This was to be a gleaming ribbon, a concrete reminder to Cambodians who traveled it through jungle and rice paddies that America was the land of know-how, can-do and will-give. It would be called the Khmer-American Friendship Highway, an enduring monument to the amity of two peoples.

The road was Cambodian ruler Prince Sihanouk's idea. The United States bought it with your tax dollars. Both got gypped. When construction began in 1956, it was estimated that the highway would cost $15 million. It was finished in 1959, a year behind schedule, and turned over to the Cambodians with much fanfare by the then Interior Secretary Fred Seaton.

Had United States-Cambodian friendship proved no more lasting than the highway, we should have been at war almost from the date of its opening. The road leaped from birth to senescence. By 1961 we had spent more than $34 million on it. And engineering reports submitted to the International Cooperation Administration, as our foreign aid agency was then called, indicated that more than a third of the two-year-old highway was already in need of major repair or complete rebuilding.

United States Ambassador to Cambodia, William C. Trimble cabled home, "I have heard from a Cambodian official that Prince Sihanouk started out on the highway a few weeks ago, but because of the condition of the highway returned and completed the trip by helicopter. The Cambodian press reported the road to be in very bad state, 'constructed without sufficient study of the climate and geologic conditions.' They added, 'The cause, in our opinion, is bad workmanship, for which the American engineers who studied the project are responsible. Hopefully, our American friends who wish to give us a solid and lasting highway will help finance its repair to maintain the reputation of American technicians.' "

The highway was to have been what our diplomats call an "impact" project—a United States status symbol. But the watchdog House Foreign Operations Subcommittee concluded that it had been so badly bungled that it had "damaged our prestige, burdened us with costly repairs, and supplied the Communists with an effective source of anti-American propaganda."

Even assuming this "friendship" road had been durably

built, was it really needed? When the first survey of the
project was made in 1955, Alvin E. Roseman, United States
Mission Director in Cambodia, was asked this question. Mr.
Roseman replied, "The principal justification was a political
justification. I would not justify this project basically as an
economic proposal. If you asked me if I would spend twenty-
five million dollars of the taxpayers' money solely on this
economic ground, I would say 'No.' "

With other members of the Foreign Operations Subcommittee, Representative Reuss visited the project while
it was under construction in November, 1957. "No question
about it, it was a splendid sight, cutting through the mountain and over the rivers of Southern Cambodia," Reuss re-
called. "Even then, though, I wondered why we were building it, in view of its probable traffic load.

"I tried to find out. No one in the Cambodian establishment of the United States seemed to know much more about
it than I. Our economic people thought it had a military
purpose. The military thought it served some economic
purpose. The most widely held view was that the road,
product of modern American methods, would be an image
of the United States in Cambodia."

The doubts of Mr. Roseman and Representative Reuss
about the highway's economic value were confirmed by a
1961 inspection of the highway by Democratic Representative Frank M. Clark of Pennsylvania, who reported, "In
the first sixty-two miles we often had to slow down for
bicycle or water-buffalo traffic. At this point we encountered
very little vehicular traffic. I learned that thirty to forty
cars and an equal number of trucks was the normal count
you could expect to see during the entire hundred-and-
thirty-mile trip. . . ."

This intelligence could hardly qualify as a surprise. The
latest available figures from the Automobile Manufacturers

Association showed that there were only 18,140 motor vehicles in all of Cambodia.

Representative Clark continued, "The shoulder areas have been allowed to become rutted, and I learned this was caused by carts pulled by water buffalo. I saw right-of-way stakes sticking up out of the rice paddies approximately a hundred feet on each side of the highway. Why, I wondered, is this encroachment of right-of-way permitted? Would not this water cause deterioration of the shoulders and eventually of the road itself?"

While the United States was busy spending on a poorly built road for buffaloes and bicycles, the Russians were wooing Cambodia with construction of a 500-bed hospital in Phnom Penh, about which more later. Commented Representative Reuss bitterly, "Russia, the master imperialist power of our century, has come into Cambodia as the benign practitioner of the healing arts. The United States, seeking only to help other peoples find themselves, has come into Cambodia bearing the prime symbol of military imperialism since Imperial Rome, the strategic highway—and a broken-down one at that."

Not everyone lost, however. The subcommittee's investigation of ICA's "inadequate, indifferent and incompetent" handling of the project indicated that the construction contractor, A. L. Dougherty Overseas, Inc., did all right. The subcommittee reported:

"All of the equipment for the project was procured by Dougherty, with ICA funds, and about a million dollars of the total was spent for used earth-moving machinery owned by Dougherty, which he purchased from himself as ICA's agent.

"This sale was with ICA's consent, but based upon certain inaccurate representations. Dougherty advised ICA that no new similar equipment was available, which was not factual. He sold the equipment to ICA at a price higher than he had been offering it to other sellers. He paid unreported commissions on the sale, contrary to ICA requirements.

"In making the sale, he transferred the equipment, without ICA knowledge, through wholly owned corporate structures, including a Liberian corporation created just for this project. This had the effect of avoiding the imposition of Federal and state income taxes on a profit which appears from Dougherty's books to have approximated $500,000."

The case of the crumbling Cambodian highway finally wound up in the lap of the U.S. Bureau of Public Roads. The Bureau was charged with determining who was at fault and to what extent. A United States Operations Mission highway engineer in Cambodia, George A. Garlinghouse, blamed faulty construction, including "incomplete soils investigation, improper embankment procedures, and improper compaction methods." ICA officials blamed it all on "unusually heavy rains."

By August, 1963, the Bureau had submitted a "confidential" report to our Agency for International Development (the latest name for our foreign aid branch), which in turn had referred it to the Justice Department to decide if there was a ground for suit.

Meanwhile, Cambodian-American friendship was being further cemented by the pouring of 6,618,240 more tax dollars into the highway between Phnom Penh and Sihanoukville. The Bureau of Public Roads took over the job of redesigning it and supervising construction. The Vinnell Corporation of Alhambra, California, was at work rebuilding or repairing the entire 132-mile link.

Apparently, our entire operation in Cambodia not only made little sense economically but contributed nothing to our political relations with that artificial little nation. At least, that was the only conclusion to be gained from the public reaction of Cambodia's Prince Sihanouk during the Diem family crisis in South Vietnam in the fall of 1963. While the United States was struggling to contain both the Communist threat and the Diem regime in that unfortunate country, the saxophone-playing Prince Sihanouk made his position crystal-clear.

"Our international policy is based on neutrality," said South Vietnam's playboy neighbor. "But should we be obliged one day to choose between [Red] China and the others, we would without hesitation choose to be on the side of the People's Republic [Communist] of China. For she alone would take the trouble to fight on our side in case of aggression from our neighbors."

Several weeks later, Sihanouk startled Foggy Bottom with an announcement that even for him was of king-size flamboyance. He decreed that all United States military and economic aid was to cease as of January 1, 1964, and that French and American troops must vacate his strategically located country. The Prince's gripe was that the United States had failed to suppress "Free Cambodian" radio stations operating clandestinely in South Vietnam and Thailand, and as punishment the United States would have to offer its handouts elsewhere. Meanwhile, Sihanouk announced he would call in five experts from Peking to help "organize state control," a move that had the international significance of putting Cambodia's head into the dragon's mouth.

However befuddled the Prince might have been in his other thinking, he was icily accurate in his estimate that as a result of ending United States aid "we will be poorer." Americans had donated $365 million to the little state since it became independent upon dissolution of French Indochina in 1954, and for fiscal 1964 AID had scheduled just under $30 million more in largesse. Sihanouk did not suggest how he was to pay for his 29,000-man army in a country still operating on a primitive-scale economy.

Apparently, however, Sihanouk believed he not only could but would be forced to do business with Communist China. He noted that "the Communists will surely triumph in South Vietnam in a few years," and added, "If we do not side with the Communists in 1963 we will have to do so in 1965 or 1966. This is inevitable." As for American foreign aid, Sihanouk's observations were similar to those made by many another charity case around the world. "Our American friends are remarkable organizers, brilliant technicians and excellent soldiers," he said. "But their incontestable realism stops short of the realm of politics, where the attitude of the ostrich seems to conform best to their interests."

Nevertheless, by the end of January, 1964, Sihanouk had agreed to discuss his differences with the United States in order to negotiate either a continuance of United States aid or its orderly phasing out. Apparently, he had forgiven us for —among other things—the Khmer-American Friendship Highway.

For all its pathetic history, the Khmer-American Friendship Highway at least was our very own. The dollars that were wasted did not go directly to finance the Communist Cold War, except by psychological accident. In the case of the Russian-financed gift of a 10-million-dollar, 500-bed hospital, mentioned earlier, American dollars in effect were spent to put the hospital on an operational basis. The House Government Operations Subcommittee was startled to discover that the hospital had been built in part with materials provided by the United States and was powered by a transformer and connecting cable bought with United States foreign aid dollars. Even worse, the subcommittee's inquiry produced no evidence that the people of Cambodia were ever informed that it was United States aid that enabled the hospital to function. "Are we to contribute our dollars to our own downfall?" the subcommittee asked. If United States handling of this situation was any indication, the answer would have to be "Yes."

This sorry saga of administrative ineptitude began on June 9, 1958, when a conscientious investigator for our Cambodian Operations Mission, Jerry M. Jackis, decided to scout out the opposition. He visited the construction site of the Russian hospital and found that American-aid cement, bearing the handclasp emblem of the ICA, was being used to build it. A tractor used on the job also bore the ICA insigne. He spotted asphalt drums with overmarkings of paint he thought might have covered the ICA emblem, and saw reinforcing steel bars he believed were probably ICA-financed.

Jackis reported his findings and recommended that the Mission Director, Alvin E. Roseman, either ask the Cambodian government to get the United States equipment off the Russian job or initiate a refund action against the Cambodian government. In a memo to the Mission's controller, Marlin F. Haas, Jackis said he did not think that "fostering and implementing of Soviet economic aid projects" was one of the objectives of our foreign aid program.

This would seem like a fair enough conclusion. But, Jackis told the subcommittee, Haas called him on the carpet and said, in effect, that he had no business snooping around the Russian hospital. Haas told the subcommittee that he and Roseman had discussed Jackis' findings but decided that since the cement and other commodities being used were apparently commodity aid, rather than material and equipment earmarked for a particular United States-aided project, there was nothing to be done about it. Jackis was rewarded for his investigative enterprise and common sense with an "unsatisfactory" efficiency rating less than a month after he wrote the memo to Haas. Two months after that he was transferred to a warehouse job and finally was dismissed despite earlier "satisfactory" and even "superior" ratings and promotions.

Subsequently, considerable Congressional pressure was applied in Jackis' behalf, particularly on the part of Senator Strom Thurmond, the fire-eating Dixiecrat from Jackis' home state of South Carolina. AID reluctantly rehired Jackis but at a lower salary, and he was assigned a desk job in which he spent most of his time working crossword puzzles for lack of anything else to do. Jackis stuck it out until October, 1963, when he resigned in a letter to AID Administrator David E. Bell, in which he charged he had been exiled to a bureaucratic Siberia because he discovered and protested against improper use of United States aid.

"It had been my hope that I would eventually be assigned once again to tasks utilizing my abilities overseas," Jackis wrote Bell. "But it is clear that the AID agency does not want a fearless investigator, even on its own staff, checking to see whether American aid is being properly used by recipient countries." Jackis noted he had been told that no "suitable" spots were open, but he added that officials told him privately that he was just "too dangerous."

Quite aside from the Jackis *cause célèbre*, it is shocking to realize that neither Washington nor our Operations Mission in Cambodia even know about use of the American-financed transformer and cable in the Russian hospital until a year after it had been installed. In designing their "showpiece," the Russians had botched the power plant. It was too small. The hospital could not operate until a large transformer to use city electric power was installed. So the Cambodian officials turned over to the Soviet project bosses an American-financed transformer and cable that had been brought in at the request of the power company in the

capital city of Phnom Penh for the stated purpose of expand-
ing the city's power facilities.

An Operations Mission auditor checking up on disposition
of the equipment a year later found and reported its installation in the hospital. He termed use of the equipment "satisfactory." The House subcommittee disagreed sharply. "The
United States Operations Mission in Cambodia, it appears,
ignored the utilization of American aid for the benefit of
the Russians, rather than cope with it," the subcommittee
snapped. "The State Department and the Agency for International Development have maintained that United States
control of goods imported under United States-financed
commodity programs is lost once the commodities enter the
country's private economy.

"AID manual orders do not require end-use checks beyond
this point, except on a selective basis, and AID officials take
the position that to check the ultimate use of all imports
would not only be a Gargantuan task, but would also con-
stitute an interference with the free-enterprise system the
United States seeks to foster. They state that for these
reasons nothing could or should have been done about the
utilization of the United States-financed commodities on the
Russian-built hospital.

"While as a general proposition there may be some merit to
their argument, it loses all validity when used as an excuse
for a failure to provide adequate safeguards to prevent the
use of United States-financed commodities to further Soviet
aims. In addition, the argument suggests that its proponents
are lacking in an understanding of the basic purposes of
the United States foreign aid program."

The subcommittee recommended that State and AID
waste no time developing regulations and procedures that
would preclude our aid henceforth from being used to

further the foreign aid activities of the Communist-bloc countries.

Uncle Sam's feckless adventures in Cambodia did produce results of a sort. For example, the Khmer-American Friendship Highway, despite its location in the mysterious East, at least boasted a pair of terminals discernible to the Occidental eye on a map. This, unhappily, is more than one can say of one of our foreign aid efforts in Peru. This was a $2 million loan for a road that would presumably open isolated areas for agricultural development and colonization. The road wound up on the side of a Peruvian mountain in the middle of nowhere.

This road was inspired by a "come-and-get-it-boys" aerogram from Washington to our aid men in Latin America. Democratic Senator George Smathers of Florida, who takes a lively interest in Latin America, had got the foreign aid act amended in 1956 to provide $52 million for South-of-the-Border aid. One portion of the Smathers amendment reserved $15 million, in part, for land resettlement programs that would advance "economic development and agricultural and industrial productivity."

Washington rushed to our field men in Latin America a request that they suggest within twenty days projects that might qualify for various programs authorized by the Smathers amendment. One of the replies came from our man in Peru, John R. Neale, then United States Operations Mission Director, proposing a road that would encourage Indians from the mountains of southern Peru to move into and farm an area called the Candamo Valley.

Eager to get these new Smathers-amendment funds nailed down, Washington approved the project and set an April 30, 1957, deadline for signing of the loan agreement. Although this deadline was met, construction did not begin until May of 1958, more than a year later.

What everyone was doing during this year-long period is not clear, but it became abundantly evident after the road was started that no one had spent any of it in intelligent planning. Moved by some sane impulse, several United States technicians belatedly journeyed into the valley for a second and more scientific look. It would, they decided, have been a dandy place to farm except for one rather important drawback. The soil was too poor.

Obviously, a "farm" road leading to untillable land would not do. So plans for the already-begun Candamo Valley road were hastily revised in favor of a more northerly route that would link it with another road, then nearing completion.

A United States rural development official who inspected the new route in April of 1959 called it "probably the roughest and most expensive road construction in Peru." At that time it was estimated that the $2 million would finance 112 kilometers. Five months later it was found that it would finance only 85 kilometers and another $2.5 million would be needed to link it with the other road.

The development official's cheerless conclusion was this: "If the road stops at kilometer 85, it will simply stop on the side of a mountain with no apparent justification of the expenditure of construction costs. . . . Before more money is advanced for the road there should be a definite field location completed to approximately kilometer 170, with a realistic and accurate cost estimate prepared, showing what the remainder of the road will cost. In addition there should be careful surveys of the proposed agriculture areas . . . which the road will serve, to determine whether there is agricultural land, timber, and other resources, in sufficient quantities, to justify the cost of the road."

House investigators who probed the case of the pointless Peruvian road closed out their findings with the discouraging report that "the road finally constructed under this loan ended in the middle of nowhere—'on the side of a mountain' —at a point about halfway along the projected route, where the project ran out of funds."

The road that went nowhere had a United States-financed counterpart in the Peruvian irrigation project that failed to irrigate. We spent $125,000 on it. The reason it did not irrigate was elementary. There was not enough water.

This was called the Pampas de Noco project. We entered into an agreement with Peru on July 26, 1956, to contribute to the project. A month later an engineer's report showed it was not feasible. Samuel Coon, then Deputy Director of the United States Operations Commission in Peru, brought the matter up again in November of 1957, urging that work be stopped. An ICA auditor also discussed it with then director Neale. He said Neale told him everybody knew the water supply was inadequate but it was necessary under Peruvian law to go ahead with the project "in order that farmers in the area might obtain clear title to the land."

Work continued until all the money was gone, and when the project was finished there still was not enough water to fill the works that were supposed to irrigate the area known as Pampas de Noco. In dollar terms, however, this abortive plan for relieving a Peruvian water shortage was a drop in the bucket compared to a mismanaged $14 million drought relief program.

The drought relief program was to have been a heart-warming demonstration of how the United States by speedy and generous gifts from its vast stores of surplus foods could help its Peruvian friends in need. It all began one March day in 1956 when both Operations Director Neale and then Ambassador Ellis O. Briggs took their respective pens in eager hands.

A fifty-day drought and early frost in the Lake Titicaca

plateau region of Peru was expected to reduce the harvest drastically, Neale advised Washington. The impact would be felt some four months hence. Ambassador Briggs backed him up: A gift of food would be in order if Neale's forecast proved correct. Two weeks later Ambassador Briggs advised that subversive elements were at work in the drought area and that without United States relief the situation could become extremely serious, resulting in social disorder and unrest.

Within the month Washington had started moving what was to total 106,000 tons of grain to Peru. Washington authorized use of the gift of grain in three ways. First, there would be a direct gift to the drought victims. Second, there would be distribution of the grain for work performed on relief projects approved jointly by the Peruvian government and the United States Operations Mission. Third, sale of the grain would be permitted if the proceeds were used to finance public works projects that would provide employment for those who lived in the drought area and would be of permanent benefit to the area.

This was the first massive dose of United States aid that Peru had received. The dosage did not kill the patient, but its administration did the doctor's reputation little good. In June of 1959 ICA sent an auditor named Frank Kemler down from Washington to find out just how our gift had been used. He spent four months trying to find out. He was only partially successful.

He did find that only 5,028 tons, or 5.7 per cent of the shipment, were actually distributed free to hungry people in the drought area. And he did learn that the rest was sold for the Peruvian equivalent of $3.6 million. Although this was permitted by terms of the Washington directive, more than 60 per cent of the sales proceeds was spent for purposes that violated the intent of the agreement. One of the glaring examples of misuse of the money was the construction of eight houses which were sold below cost on the installment plan to prominent persons in the town of Puno.

Although the grain was first sold at or below current market prices, a third of it, 35,000 tons, was sold to Peruvian millers who then resold almost all of it through normal commercial channels. And 28,000 of these 35,000 tons were sold to a single mill that was outside of the drought area. Reported Auditor Kemler, "We could not determine the quantity of the food sold through normal commercial channels that actually reached or did not reach drought victims."

The Peruvian government declared the drought officially ended on May 15, 1958. As of that date 25,000 tons of the grain still had not been distributed, and it was not until March 7, 1960, that it had all been finally disposed of. Kemler concluded that "either more food was requested than was needed for the program, or the food was not distributed to the drought victims in an effective and timely manner."

Why was this program, meant to help hungry people and add luster to our image in Latin America, so badly botched? Coon, the former Deputy Director of the Peruvian Operations Mission under Neale, had complained to ICA's Latin American Operations office in May, 1958, about mismanagement of this and other projects in Peru. But it was not until after he had voiced his complaints before a Congressional appropriations subcommittee that the story really began unfolding.

The House Foreign Operations Subcommittee, then headed by Democratic Representative Porter Hardy, Jr., of Virginia, began digging in. Kemler's report and other ICA documents were spread on the record. ICA officials were called in to testify. The picture finally rounded out by the subcommittee and reported to Congress in 1961 was this:

Although Ambassador Briggs had warned that Peruvian

officials had neither the experience nor the facilities to handle such a big program, Neale had turned it over to them almost entirely. Washington was not advised about this. Nor did Neale bother to get prior Washington approval of projects proposed by the Peruvian government that were to be financed with proceeds from sale of the grain. This was contrary to Washington's instructions at the time of the gift.

Also without authority from Washington, Neale had told the Peruvian government to charge off what it had spent to administer the drought relief program as though the money was spent for work relief. This violated the agreement between the United States and Peru that Peru was to bear the administrative expenses of the program. It also substantially reduced the amount of money available to help the drought-area victims.

Neale had been with ICA and its predecessors for fifteen years, most of the time as a Mission Director, and had presided over the United States aid program in Peru almost from its start. He was finally asked to resign and did so on June 30, 1958, because of a conflict of interest. It was charged he had helped organize and had invested in a corporation called Negociación Bazo Velarde, S.A., a farming operation which was receiving aid under the United States program. He had not bothered to advise his superiors in Washington about this little sideline.

The subcommittee leaned hardest on Neale, recommending administrative action that would prevent directors and other key overseas personnel from "becoming entrenched, as Neale did when director in Peru." But it spread the blame liberally. Ambassador Theodore C. Achilles, who succeeded Briggs, "demonstrated important gaps in his knowledge of the activities of his subordinates."

Rollins S. Atwood, who was regional director of the Office of Latin American Operations, "failed to take corrective action" even when he had "adequate basis for questioning the quality of the administration of the aid program in Peru." Within the aid branch itself the subcommittee found inadequate audit procedures and considerable foot dragging by agency investigators "where prompt and adequate investigation might have proved embarrassing to ICA, the United States Operations Mission, or to Neale."

One of the unsung heroes of the grain relief scandal was a man named Roger Stewart, chief of the Cereals Branch of ICA's Office of Food and Agriculture. He became aware about September of 1957 that the program was being maladministered and urged that an accounting of funds be demanded. It took him until December to get even the draft of a message to Neale approved. Stewart said the Peruvian desk officer, a friend of Neale's, fought him, and in a letter tipping Neale off that Stewart's demands would prevail wrote that "barrages between us have been anything but pleasant."

It belongs to the thesis of this book that Stewart and two of the other men who helped blow the whistle on the wasteful use of your foreign aid money in Peru were officials or employees of the foreign agency itself—Coon, the former Deputy Director of the Peruvian Mission, and Auditor Kemler. This point is central to the writers' belief that the most conscientious concern for the productive use of our tax dollars by administrators and executive employees themselves is a prerequisite for the survival of a meaningful foreign aid program.

Since World War II, the United States has spent more than $100 billion on foreign aid of one kind or another. However official Washington may blithely toss such figures about, this is a great deal of money. It is difficult to understand just how much it is, but it helps to bring it down to earth by remembering that it is more than twice the assessed valuation, real and otherwise, in the nation's thirteen largest cities:

New York, Chicago, Los Angeles, Philadelphia, Detroit, Baltimore, Houston, Cleveland, Washington, St. Louis, Milwaukee, San Francisco, and Boston.

In other words, we have given to the world in the last twenty-two years twice the equivalent of our thirteen largest cities, according to the 1960 census.

Foreign aid has served us well. Massive infusions of our money, imagination and planning leadership inoculated a weakened Western Europe against the virus of communism following World War II. Greece and Turkey were saved by our guns and dollars from Moscow-directed infiltrations. More recently, emerging African nations, uncertain of their place in world affairs, have at least been kept from offering themselves as willing morsels to the Russian Bear.

With the ebbing of such immediate dangers to our friends as direct Communist attack or total economic collapse, the role of our aid program understandably became both more complex and less apparent. But we would agree with the late President Kennedy that "the United States—the richest and most powerful of all peoples, a nation committed to the independence of nations and to a better life for all peoples—can no more stand aside in this climactic age of decision than we can withdraw from the community of free nations. Our effort is not merely symbolic. It is addressed to our vital security interests."

In 1963, Frank M. Coffin, Deputy Administrator for Operations of the Agency for International Development, had this to say about the program's contribution to our security: "What happens in Argentina, sub-Sahara Africa, or Afghanistan may not measurably lessen our security today, tomorrow, or next year. If Southeast Asia were to be sucked into the Communist orbit, Main Street, U.S.A., might not today be visibly affected.

"But the power of the free world would have significantly

diminished. An historic retreat would have begun. Our children and our children's children would live in a narrower, more constricted, more threatening world. When we recognize that we are thinking of the generations that follow us, 'security' becomes synonymous with 'liberty.' Our vision of long-term security is a vision of a world where the boundaries of freedom are advancing, not retreating."

Most Americans today would readily agree. When asked simply if they are "for" or "against" foreign aid, 60 per cent of our people reply "for." Yet the program has come under increasingly heavy attack from a very special group of Americans—the ones who must vote the money to keep it going. These are the members of the United States Congress. And, significantly, the attack comes not just from the Congressional right wings of both parties, but even from such recognized liberals as Representative Reuss and Democratic Senators Wayne Morse of Oregon, Frank Church of Idaho and Ernest Gruening of Alaska.

Legislators may and do properly ask just how the present or future national interests of the United States are served by a badly built and costly Cambodian road or a Peruvian irrigation system that lacks water. The obvious answer is that they are not.

It is easy to observe, since it has proved unhappily true, that a nation that has spent more than $100 billion since World War II to help its neighbors must have miscalculated and misspent more than a few times. But it is also true that a nation so big of heart and broad of vision has an obligation to both itself and its friends to husband its resources and spend them only in ways that will neither dissipate its own strength nor sully its reputation in the world community.

America's own impatience and irritation with foreign aid is more frequently reflected in the simple declarative protests of the man in the street in Dubuque or Seattle, or in the angry oratory of the fundamentalist legislator on the floor of the House or the Senate. But it also causes frustration at much more sophisticated levels. During a speech before the Economic Club in New York in December, 1962, even the man who was required to champion a $4.9 billion request for more help to the needy nations was frankly fretful.

"I would like to cut out foreign aid," said President Kennedy. "It is very unpopular. It is a hard fight every year. President Eisenhower had the same struggle, and so did President Truman." But in the next moment he was admitting—with most of the rest of America—that it was a fact of Cold-War life that had to be lived with.

Kennedy, of course, was a hard-boiled pragmatist in international affairs. What was more revealing was the about-face of that professional do-gooder and friend of the international downtrodden, Chester Bowles. By the summer of 1962, the harassing complexities of foreign aid had so penetrated the liberal camp that Bowles was suggesting a complete reappraisal of the entire foreign aid operation. Bowles recommended that the program be regeared to the principle of "selectivity," so that countries making a sincere effort to improve their economies would be given priority. With the pitiless candor of a Robert A. Taft, Bowles declared it was time to abandon, or put at the tail end of the handout list, those countries which were either unable or unwilling to make an honest woman of their society.

Like Atlas of old, the United States holds the world on its shoulders, or at least that portion of the world which is free or neutral. The financial burden is heavy. The responsibility for freedom is awesome. The irony of our situation is that only a few short decades ago the young giant, absorbed with its own growth and development, was not only willing but insistent that management of the world stage should be the responsibility of others. So it is with genuine astonishment that many an American taxpayer today, on learning that he has paid for a radio station in Vietnam or a dam in the Middle East or an Ethiopian Emperor's yacht, asks, "How did we get into *this* business?"

2 *From Caesar to Lyndon Johnson*

It is necessary to an understanding of the American foreign aid program to go back to history. For, from an historical standpoint, it was inevitable that the United States should have got into a business which, down through the years, has proved to be an occupational disease of great powers. From Harry Truman, Dwight D. Eisenhower and John F. Kennedy, President Lyndon Johnson inherited the program as one of the necessities of that fact of life known as the Cold War.

Imperial Rome had the disease, but treated it in a way that the American taxpayer today might envy. The Empire's military aid program guaranteed the sovereignty of Rome's weaker neighbors in return for a share of the neighbor's wealth. This, of course, smacked somewhat of the "protection racket" later practiced by American gangland and obviously would offend the sensibilities of today's diplomat. The United States often makes the same guarantees for much less negotiable returns.

In the seventeenth and eighteenth centuries, great Western powers like England and France furnished troops, food and money to their allies and made loans in exchange for military manpower to protect their mutual interests. Furthermore they did not ignore the refreshingly direct device of the out-and-out bribe. Thus, Sir Henry Wotton, British Ambassador to Venice in the seventeenth century, accepted a "pension" from Savoy while applying to Spain for another. Good Queen Bess's Minister to Spain, Lord Robert Cecil, got a Spanish pension. France spent 82 million livres to buy the favors of Austrian statesmen in the eighteenth century. And fledgling America's first Congress in 1789 included in its first appropriation act a modest contingent fund for just such discreetly administered "foreign aid."

Political scientist Hans Morgenthau of the University of Chicago argues, in fact, that bribery as a tool of diplomacy is not dead—just disguised. "Much of what goes by the name of foreign aid today is in the nature of bribes," he contends. "The transfer of money and services from one government to another performs here the function of a price paid for political services rendered or to be rendered. . . .

"They are justified primarily in terms of foreign aid for economic development, and money and services are transferred through elaborate machinery fashioned for genuine economic aid. In consequence, these bribes are a less effective means for the purpose of purchasing political favors than were the traditional ones. . . . Old-fashioned bribery was a relatively straightforward transaction; services were to be rendered at a price, and both sides knew what to expect. Bribery disguised as foreign aid for economic development makes of giver and recipient actors in a play, which in the end they may no longer be able to distinguish from reality.

"In consequence, both may come to expect results in terms of economic development which in the nature of things may not be forthcoming. Thus both are likely to be disappointed, the giver blaming the recipient for his inefficiency and the recipient accusing the giver of stinginess and asking for more. The ideology, if taken for reality, gets in the way of the original purpose of the transaction, and neither side believes that it has received what it is entitled to."

The American people, however, had few if any reservations about the value to them of the transaction that marked the birth of our massive aid program. This was the World War II gift to Britain of fifty overage destroyers in trade for American bases on eight British North American possessions. It was announced on September 3, 1940. In comparison to our later lavish giving, that was indeed a modest beginning. And it was widely applauded.

For this was the time when the few to whom so many owed so much were battling in the air over Britain. The Axis war machine was in high gear. America, as yet unprepared to intervene in Europe's war for the second time in barely two decades, watched uneasily as Hitler's Panzer divisions sped almost at will throughout Western Europe, and the hobnailed boots of dictatorship seemed to be beating out a dirge for democracy.

Even under these circumstances, however, President Franklin D. Roosevelt was so uncertain of Congressional reaction to the destroyer deal that he accomplished it by Executive order. In the preceding June, Congress had amended the Naval appropriations bill to permit the Chief Executive to transfer property if the Chief of Staff or Chief of Naval Operations first certified it was not needed for United States defense. Adm. Harold R. Stark, then Chief of Naval Operations, certified that the destroyers were unneeded in view of the increased strength we would derive from having acquired the bases.

This popular move to help our British friends paved the way for Congressional passage the following year of the Lend-Lease Act, under which we would lease military equipment to "any country whose defense the President deems vital to the defense of the United States." This much broader program, giving the President vast powers to distribute at his discretion American tax dollars worldwide, drew considerable opposition.

But Roosevelt was at the height of his popularity, and arguments for the program were compelling. It permitted us to maintain a technical neutrality while sustaining with arms and equipment the allies beside whom we would within months be fighting a global war. The Senate gave it a two-to-one vote of approval. In March, 1941, Congress authorized the President to spend $7 billion on lend-lease— a figure that was to grow to $42,020,779,261 before the program was closed out. On December 7, 1941, the Japanese made their sneak attack on Pearl Harbor. Any substantial doubts about the wisdom of having voted lend-lease into being ended abruptly. We were fighting for our lives, and money did not matter much then.

The United States, of course, had made earlier and more cautious ventures into the business of helping its friends. During the First World War we had sent money abroad, but on a loan basis. After our recognition of Communist Russia in 1933, we set up the Export-Import Bank, originally intended as an agency to help promote United States–Russian trade. Although it failed to achieve this purpose, the bank did grow into a worldwide operation and has prospered on a self-liquidating basis.

But it was lend-lease, a win-the-war program, and its open-handed administration, that set the pattern of worldwide largesse America was to follow in the postwar period. As it has turned out, to no one's particular surprise, the "lend-lease" moniker was somewhat misleading. Only a small fraction of our $42 billion has ever been recovered.

Even today, the State Department is inclined to be vague

about just how much has been repaid; its excuse for its evasiveness is that so much of what little was recovered has been lost in the jungle of accounting concerned with local-currency support of American installations abroad. In 1953, the figure was $48,374,745 in hard American dollars; since then there has been no really dependable total available. The fact is that neither the Truman nor the Eisenhower administrations felt it worthwhile to press for repayment because of the sentimental peculiarities of the fine print governing the "loans." During the war, Uncle Sam did his best to avoid creating the impression he was a mere money lender, and as a result, wartime administrators of the program dispensed much of the aid without restrictions or any clear understanding that the money being poured out was, in fact, a loan rather than a giveaway.

One Col. Igor Bogolepov, former counselor of the Russian Foreign Office, for instance, told the Senate Internal Security Subcommittee in 1952 about a 1941 visit to Moscow by Harry L. Hopkins, President Roosevelt's lend-lease envoy. Stalin, said the colonel, had prepared for the Hopkins visit by having the then Foreign Minister V. M. Molotov head a committee to draft a series of maximum concessions that Russia would make in return for lend-lease help. They would, he said, have permitted Americans behind Soviet lines, American inspection of lend-lease materials used, opening of Siberia to American investment, manganese mining concessions to Americans, and granting of civil liberties to the Russian people. To the surprise and delight of Stalin and Company, Hopkins never even asked for such concessions. Bogolepov, of course, was a defector and this is a tribe which likes to tell tales its audience wants to hear. But his testimony was credible when placed in the context of our wartime enthusiasm for helping anybody who was fighting Adolf Hitler. Our lavish gifts of goods helped us achieve our immediate goal, the winning of the war. Had they been more prudently bestowed, however, they might also have helped us win the peace. Many of the political problems that plague us in today's Cold War might have been precluded by more hardheaded and farsighted negotiation with Russia and other wartime allies for our lend-lease aid. Assuming that this failure could be excused amid the chaos and tragedy of the greatest war in history, one would still like to think that it had at least served as a lesson for the future. But has it?

Over twenty-one years, four Presidents and eleven Congresses had supported foreign aid programs in which over $100 billion had been spent for relief, foods and supplies, military aid, grants, development loans and technical assistance. Had we learned over this period how to use our foreign aid effectively? Writing in the *American Political Science Review* of June, 1962, political scientist Morgenthau answered "No":

As it has developed in recent years, the kind [of foreign aid policy] we have is fundamentally weak. It has been conceived as a self-sufficient technical enterprise, covering a multitude of disparate objectives and activities, responding haphazardly to all sorts of demands, sound and unsound, unrelated or only by accident related to the political purposes of our foreign policy. The United States, in short, has been in the business of foreign aid for more than two decades, but it has yet to develop an intelligible theory of foreign aid that could provide standards of judgment for both the supporters and opponents of a particular measure.

But this book is not an argument for abandonment of our foreign aid effort. That would be the ultimate waste. It would be throwing a $100 billion baby out with the bath water. It would mistakenly presuppose that because the means was too often wasteful the end should be abandoned. The end purpose of the program is simply to manipulate affairs so that Americans can live peaceably and productively in a highly volatile world. Despite the extremes of emotion that foreign aid provokes, it is, as a foreign policy device, neither "good" nor "bad." It is, instead, either successful or unsuccessful, either advancing or impeding the self-interest of the people who pay for it, the American taxpayers.

Its champions argue—successfully, we think—that foreign aid is an important instrument in our diplomatic tool kit, even though it is not needed for our immediate national survival. There is no single nation save Russia that we could not conquer with comparative impunity by force of nuclear arms. But Russia's development of its own vast arsenal has created a nuclear stalemate, the breaking of which would result in such horror that, as the late President Kennedy and Soviet Premier Khrushchev agreed, the victor would envy the vanquished dead.

In this stalemated situation the jockeying of the two great powers has moved more and more into the economic and political arena, with each trying to keep the other from acquiring controlling influence over strategic areas as yet uncommitted to either camp. Should one camp succeed so completely that the other was economically and politically isolated, force of arms might not then be needed to dominate the loser. This, apparently, was what Soviet Premier Khrushchev meant by his "We will bury you" prediction.

This is the shape of a world in which bits and pieces must be fitted together if we are to survive. Whatever tools—military, political or economic—are needed for the job must be provided. But the careful workman understands the use of his tools and tolerates no abuse of them. He does not use a hammer when an awl is required, or vice versa. The United States, unhappily, has too often been less than careful of its foreign aid tools and has sometimes wielded them with such clumsiness that it has hammered its own finger.

The blasé attitude of bureaucracy exemplified by the Cambodian hospital deal has been unhappily apparent at many points along the path our aid commitments have traveled since World War II. With the pattern of casual administration already established by lend-lease, our handling of postwar relief was likewise too often marked more by noble impulse than by thoughtful purpose.

For example, Russia also profited undeservedly from operations of the United Nations Relief and Rehabilitation Administration (UNRRA), which we bankrolled in major part. UNRRA undertook the laudable humanitarian task of feeding, clothing and housing the millions left destitute in war's wake. But because these gifts, largely paid for by American taxpayers, were doled out in Eastern Europe through Moscow-controlled *de facto* governments, the Russian Bear was presented to its political victims as a gift-laden lamb. This contrasted sharply with the vast harvest of good will America itself reaped in Europe after World War I, when Herbert Hoover, later to become President of the United States, directed a relief program financed in large part by private contributions.

Even today, despite our own huge unilateral foreign aid commitments, we continue to bear a disproportionately large share of some United Nations costs—a fact that a blue-ribbon panel of the late President Kennedy's own choosing deplored in a report to him on March 20, 1963. This was the report of the "Committee to Strengthen the Security of the Free World," popularly known as the Clay committee after its chairman, soldier-statesman Gen. Lucius D. Clay. Kennedy, of course, had packed the Clay committee with conservatives and big businessmen, and there were many critics who moaned that its makeup precluded any impartial judgment of the aid program. But, after all, big business is one of the chief beneficiaries of foreign aid, and the authors believe that it is valuable to an understanding of foreign aid to give a hearing from time to time to the committee's views.

"United States contributions to the budgets [of United Nations assistance agencies] should not exceed our proportionate share of our regular UN assessment," the Clay committee said. "Exceptions should be limited to contributions designed to increase the totals of these budgets proportionately and should be discontinued promptly if they fail in this purpose." Our maximum share of the regular United Nations budget is 33⅓ per cent. But for some special United Nations programs we contribute from 40 to 100 per cent, even though some of the aid goes to Communist-bloc countries. Complained Republican Representative Durward G. Hall of Missouri during debate on the fiscal 1964 foreign aid authorization bill:

"The Soviet Union contributes no more to the [United Nations] special fund now than she did in 1959. Her pledge each year is for $1 million—less than the contribution of tiny Switzerland. Yet, the United States contribution to the special fund has grown from $10 million in 1959 to $29 million in 1963, an increase of almost 300 per cent. If benefit nations do not criticize Russia for paying less than its fair share, surely no one nation can criticize the United States for not paying more than its fair share."

Uncle Sam, however, has never been overly worried about contributing more than his "fair share," as other postwar programs attested. Billions of dollars were spent by our Armed Forces Civilian Supply Program, a humanitarian effort to help the people we had conquered and restore social order in occupied Japan and West Germany. Congress also appropriated $600 million to help Austria, Italy and France with their postwar problems.

But it was with the Truman Doctrine, unveiled on March 12, 1947, that we began to weave massive aid into the perma-

nent fabric of our postwar conduct of foreign affairs. The
doctrine pledged our help to free peoples threatened by
totalitarian regimes. It marked the advent of our Cold War
with Russia. Under it, we rushed hundreds of millions of
dollars in arms and military advisers to Greece and arms and
economic help to Turkey and succeeded in forestalling
threatened Russian encroachments. The Truman Doctrine
was the first in a series of programs, initiated more or less in
response to Soviet threat or provocation. It was followed almost immediately by what was perhaps the best-conceived
and most successfully executed economic aid program in
world history.

Secretary of State George C. Marshall first told the world
about it on June 5, 1947. In a speech at Harvard University,
which had conferred an honorary Doctor of Laws degree on
him, the former five-star general said, "It would be neither
fitting nor efficacious for this government to draw up unilat-
erally a program designed to place Europe on its feet economically. This is the business of Europeans. The initiative,
I think, must come from Europe. The role of this country
should consist of friendly aid in the drafting of a European
program and of later supporting such a program so far as it
may be practical for us to do so. The program should be a
joint one agreed to by a number, if not all European nations."

Thus was born the four-year Marshall Plan, a timely, if
costly, venture which would restore war-ravaged Europe and
snatch from Communism the opportunity to convert poverty
and misery into Marxist gains, particularly in Italy and
France. Administered by what was then called our Economic
Cooperation Administration (ECA), we invested some $13
billion, all but 14 per cent in outright grants. Spurred by the
condition that American aid must be earned by European
planning initiative, the Old World quickly climbed to new
heights of prosperity. The spirit of European cooperation

engendered by the Marshall Plan led to the creation of the European Coal and Steel Community in 1952 and, finally, in 1957 to the European Economic Community—the now rich and growing Common Market. Had Europe remained impoverished, divided and susceptible to Communist political subversion, the position of the United States today might be infinitely more difficult and dangerous.

The Marshall Plan's success, however, was attributable to several factors absent from President Truman's next economic aid proposal. Point Four in his 1949 inaugural address was a plan to offer United States technicians, equipment and capital to help underdeveloped countries, as we continue to do today. Many a grumbler about our aid to underdeveloped countries was a willing champion of the Marshall Plan. The differences are that aid to Europe was for recovery, rather than development. Europe had the governmental experience, the managerial know-how and the skilled manpower to use it effectively. Results were apparent, gratifying and in our obvious self-interest. Whether wealthy Europe, in turn, has since shouldered its own fair share of the burden of sustaining freedom is a matter of current debate.

But even the 1949 Point Four program was more modest in its original reach than today's efforts. It was to be, as then Secretary of State Dean Acheson told Congress, an effort "to show other people how to meet their own needs, not to attempt to meet those needs ourselves." At the close of the Truman administration, technical assistance costs had totaled some $68 million. Now they run about $315 million a year.

Another program was born in 1949 following Russian efforts to blockade our war-won right to presence in Berlin. This was the North Atlantic Treaty Organization, the predominantly defensive alliance through which the United States and her Western allies would "shield" themselves from Soviet military ambitions. Besides our own contributions of men and equipment, the Mutual Defense Assistance Act of 1949 committed us to supplying such arms and equipment to our NATO allies as they could not finance themselves. The economic and defense burden of this new venture was predominantly ours, and remains so today.

By 1951 we were trying to coordinate our vast economic and military programs under the three-year Mutual Security Administration. This effort at coordination has continued. During the Eisenhower years our aid-administering agency was reorganized and variously called the Foreign Operations Administration (1953–55) and the International Cooperation Administration. The Kennedy administration reorganized and renamed it the Agency for International Development.

Under President Eisenhower the surplus food distribution program began, and there was invented a new form of economic aid known as defense support. It provided that the United States would support the military establishments of various friendly but impecunious regimes on the periphery of the Eurasian continent. It was part of the late Secretary of State John Foster Dulles' "containment" theory that as these nations circling the Communist bloc were armed and Europe grew stronger, United States forces could be brought home. So we began absorbing the costs of pay, uniforms, housing and even foreign exchange deficits of our poorer friends.

Meanwhile, on the economic aid front, the Eisenhower administration sought to counter Congressional criticism of foreign "giveaways" by developing agencies for the administration of loans, some of them so "soft" that they practically amounted to grants. These included such international lending agencies as the Development Loan Fund (DLF), offering long-term, extra-low-interest-rate loans to nations that could not qualify at the World Bank; the International Development Association (IDA), a kind of "soft-loan window" at the

World Bank; and the Inter-American Development Bank (IDB) to serve Latin America with both hard- and soft-loan services.

Most of the programs over the years have been presented as temporary. Strategic justifications for them have been redefined. The proportion of military versus economic aid has fluctuated as crises flared or died out. (Since war's end through fiscal 1962 we had distributed some $31 billion in military aid, less than half of what we spent for economic aid, which was $66.6 billion. Only 35.9 per cent of the economic aid was through loans.) But the result over the years has been the same—more foreign aid outlays. One hundred nine foreign countries or territories have benefited. AID as of 1963 was directly hiring 15,000 persons to distribute our largesse, about 13,000 of them serving overseas, and employing another 2,000 persons abroad under contract.

3 *Solar Boats and TV Sets*

On paper it would appear that Uncle Sam's 17,000
AID employees must exercise the utmost care in bestowing
the taxpayers' billions upon less favored countries. But the not
very sunny case of the solar-powered boat and the dim picture presented by a deal for 1,000 transistorized television
sets indicate that this is not universally so. Before discussing
in detail such depressing adventures in foreign aid, however,
it seems meet to examine the circumstances concerning the
birth and upbringing of a typical AID project. Contrary to
some cynics, the United States Treasury does not hold periodic open houses at which foreign governments are invited
to help themselves to our money. It merely seems that way.

It might start during breakfast in Bangkok, lunch in Lima
or dinner in New Delhi, with a local official's suggestion to
our AID representative there that Uncle Sam's image would
be considerably brightened by the gift of anything from a
bathhouse to a yacht—we have contributed both. Our AID
man says, "Draw up a blueprint and we'll have a look." The
blueprint, outlining the project and the kind of aid needed
to carry it out, is submitted to the AID mission, which is
attached to our Embassy.

Mission officials look it over from an economic view. If the project is of the icebox-for-Eskimos variety, they, presumably, reject it. The United States Ambassador examines its political implications. If it will make Mao Tse-tung sleep better of nights, the Ambassador, presumably, will quash it. But if they agree it is a good one, they send it on to Washington for a review by a desk officer in charge of the country involved.

If the desk officer likes it, he bumps it on up to a regional administrator. As reorganized by the Foreign Assistance Act of September, 1961, the Washington headquarters is run by four regional bureaus: Latin America; Far East; Near East and South Asia; and Africa and Europe. Each regional bureau is headed by an Assistant Administrator with the rank of Assistant Secretary of State. If the regional administrator approves of the project, he sends it on to the Administrator for final O.K.

But this is just how the project gets up the hill. It also has to get back down. Congress sometimes makes the descent difficult. Planning of projects on a country-by-country basis begins some fifteen months before the President's budget is submitted. Programs based on what AID has asked for later have to be retailored in terms of what it has received from Congress, which has displayed a growing tendency to pare foreign aid funds.

An AID program for a given country is subject from its very conception to a series of tugs-of-war. First, there is the pulling and hauling between the State Department and the Pentagon over the sometimes separate but usually entangled programs of economic and military aid. The State Department's first interest, of course, is the long-range political goal. It will sacrifice tactical advantage for strategic gain in the field of ideology. The Defense Department wants to make our friends militarily strong enough to contain and defeat its enemies on the battlefield, on the theory that the way for a nation to maintain or achieve its independence is to be stronger than the Communists in the shooting department. Put in the simplest of terms, the Pentagon is interested in winning today's battle lest it lose two more tomorrow, while State must consider the developing problems that will be posed ten years from now. Possibly because this is a government of civilians, State usually exerts the most influence on the AID program, although there are exceptions—such as in Formosa, where the diplomats have unsuccessfully bucked the military's demands for a garrison far more powerful than Chiang Kai-shek's political influence in the Far East would warrant.

Within the State Department, too, there are rivalries between the assistant secretaries representing the interests of the Far East, the Middle East, Africa and Latin America. Each tries to get as much money for his part of the world as he can manage, usually at the expense of the others. And in Congress, of course, any legislator may propose and force passage of an amendment taking AID money away from one country and giving it to another. Indeed, it is on Capitol Hill where most of the restrictions on foreign aid are born, as in the case of Senator Mundt's amendment forbidding United States guarantees of wheat loans to Communist countries.

If the project survives the battle of the budget and is undertaken, its conduct is then the subject of considerable review. On the scene there is a so-called "end-use" investigator attached to our overseas Mission. He reports directly to the AID controller in Washington on how the project is going. A Management Inspection Staff in Washington also looks over the Mission Director's shoulder. The General Accounting Office, independent watchdog over Executive spending, and various Congressional committees make periodic checks, too.

But within an agency with billions of dollars to spend there is apparently a tendency to regard the abuse of mere tens of thousands of tax dollars as something less than waste. The House Foreign Operations Subcommittee turned up an example of this in, of all places, a division of AID especially created to find ways to make more efficient use of our aid dollars. Established by general notice December 29, 1961, it was called the Research, Evaluation and Planning Assistance Staff (REPAS). Before the subcommittee stepped in, it was about to originate an inefficient project of its own. The story, as described by the subcommittee, was this:

A $35-a-day AID communications consultant named John Hoke wanted to cruise up and down the rivers of the little South American country of Surinam in a sun-powered boat. Hoke had formerly been employed by AID's predecessor (ICA) and had been stationed in Surinam as a "communications media officer." While there he had written a story for the National Geographic Society about the three-toed sloth, which also lives in Surinam, and had become interested in solar cells. After he left ICA in 1961, he had tried to get electronics companies to supply boat, equipment, solar cells and salary; to get the Army to finance the expedition; and to get the National Geographic Society interested in covering it. No luck.

Shortly before AID hired Hoke on January 22, 1962, however, the Hoffman Electronics Corporation of El Monte, California, had shown some interest in Hoke's idea. But after Hoke joined AID "he appears to have changed his strategy and sought to obtain financing by the government instead of private industry," the subcommittee concluded after hearings. Hoke succeeded. On May 25, 1962, AID contracted with Hoffman for a collapsible boat, propulsion system, and 100-watt panel of solar cells for $28,625. The expedition was apparently in business. By cruising the rivers of Surinam it was to "test performance of solar-powered battery-recharging centers for communications equipment and various other low-wattage powered tools (winch, drills, pumping equipment, etc.) and focus attention on the peacetime terrestrial uses of solar power so as to generate demand and motivation for privately financed research and development programs designed rapidly to reduce the cost of solar cells."

During his solar-powered boat campaign Hoke kept in close touch with Hoffman Electronics "and from the wording of some of his letters one would have difficulty in deciding whether Hoke was working for AID or Hoffman Electronics," the subcommittee found. "He at least gave the impression of being predominantly occupied with the interests of the latter." Nor did he forget his National Geographic friends. They wanted to send a photographer along on this government-supported venture and offered Hoke payment for a manuscript if he produced one they could use.

The same day subcommittee investigators began asking AID officials about Hoke's tie-up with the National Geographic, he wrote to the magazine saying that "there need be no remuneration" for any story he might write, but that if there was a "token honorarium" it would go to the Agency.

Assuming that the sun-powered boat test would, in fact, be a useful taxpayer-financed research and demonstration project, why would the taxpayer have to bankroll a costly expedition to Surinam to carry it out? The sun also shines on the Potomac River, which flows practically at the doorstep of AID headquarters in Washington's Foggy Bottom area. After the House subcommittee's pointed queries, the contract was held up. The latest report was that AID decided it was really not a bad idea and recommended going ahead with the Hoffman contract. But AID canceled its Surinam expedition and turned the testing over to the United States Army Electronic Research and Development Laboratories at

Fort Monmouth, New Jersey. These tests will not cost AID a cent.

The dim picture of the television transaction flickered on in June, 1962. It, too, presented a view of AID's idea of efficiency—as seen through a glass darkly. Dr. Gerald F. Winfield, chief of AID's communications resources division, advised REPAS that an "urgent requirement has been established for the purchase of 1,000 transistorized special 23-inch television sets employing fiscal year 1962 REPAS funds in the amount of $400,000." He asked that purchase of the sets be negotiated with Warwick Manufacturing Company, Chicago, as the sole source of such equipment. The contract was signed on June 29, the last working day of the fiscal year.

In its probe of this contract the House subcommittee made it clear that it was not criticizing the idea behind it. In some eighty countries abroad where AID conducts educational programs, there are 250 million school-age children not in school and some 500 million adult illiterates. Television would be a good teaching tool, particularly if it was used on a community basis. The specialized sets would be set up in villages that were within receiving distance of a television transmitting station but without adequate local power to operate a regular AC-DC set.

But why the sudden rush to order the sets? Illiteracy among the peoples of underdeveloped countries was not exactly a startlingly new discovery; why not ask for bids, which usually insure a better bargain than negotiated contracts? And was there really only one possible source of supply? After weighing the testimony it had heard, the subcommittee reported, "Unfortunately, Winfield does not know where or specifically how these sets are to be used. And unfortunately for the taxpayer, the amount authorized for the purchase of the television receivers does not include the costs of generators, charging devices, antennas and spare

parts. The cost of these, according to Winfield, will be an
additional $729,500. Further costs of delivery, testing of
equipment, and developing general plans and prototype materials for testing television educational programs in the field
will bring the total projected cost of this program to over
$1.6 million.

"Mr. Winfield was able to rush the purchase of the television sets through AID on the representation that there was
an 'urgent requirement' for the receivers. Apparently no one
seriously questioned his judgment. In his testimony before
the subcommittee, however, he admitted that a significant
part of this urgency stemmed from the fact that the funds
had to be obligated before the end of the fiscal year—that is,
by June 30, 1962. Otherwise, the funds would revert to the
United States Treasury."

Obviously the bureaucratic horror of not spending far exceeded any compunctions about prudent expenditure of the
tax dollar. The contract for the television sets was entered
into with such haste that the AID negotiator even forgot to
include the standard termination clause. The subcommittee
found that tests on the equipment contracted for were "limited to observation of picture quality and casual inspection
of the set by AID personnel with no experience or compe-
tence to make any technical evaluation." The set so casually
inspected was a prototype model and not yet in production.

At one point in the subcommittee hearing, then Chairman
Porter Hardy asked, "Who tested the Warwick set?" Replied
Dr. Winfield, "No one." Asked Representative Hardy, "So
you bought it without testing?" Dr. Winfield replied, "Yes,
sir." Furthermore, the subcommittee developed testimony
that Warwick was not, in fact, the sole source of supply and
that the taxpayers' investment could have been better protected by inviting some competition for the business. Motor-
ola would have provided sets of the same specifications for

$141 less per set than the price hastily negotiated with War-
wick—a $141,000 saving lost because, the subcommittee con-
cluded, "the employees involved failed to follow established
procedures or exercise reasonable diligence." Latest word on
this bit of bungling was that after the subcommittee exposed
it, the contract had been closed out and investigation was
under way to determine whether it would cost the government anything.

Over the years, foreign aid has been plagued by so much
of this perfunctory, careless and ill-informed spending that
it is a near miracle it has not been destroyed by the outrage
of Main Street. From Iraq to Korea, it sometimes has seemed
that Uncle Sam was spending his dollars in a kind of despera-
tion, as though he was afraid they would go out of style.

In South Korea, the taxpayers paid the salaries and expenses of a corps of American experts dispatched to teach
the Koreans how to grow more rice. And yet the per-acre
production of rice in Korea was already many times the
per-acre production in Louisiana, where modern methods
were used.

At one time or another, foreign aid:

Paid for free airplane excursions for thousands of Arabs
visiting the Moslem shrine at Mecca.

Financed a fifteen-mile, six-lane highway connecting the
Portuguese capital of Lisbon with the gambling resort of
Estoril.

Paid for a "psychological" project in the Netherlands for
the purpose of studying the behavior of the Dutch.

Built a silica plant in Formosa at the cost of more than
$150,000, which operated for thirty days and then closed
down because of a lack of silica.

Built four wheat-flour mills in South Korea although no
wheat was grown in that country at the time.

Paid the tuition costs and living expenses for the sons of

hundreds of wealthy Iranians attending American universities and colleges.

Built an Italian village that nobody could be persuaded to live in.

It is this kind of waste of time, manpower and money that gives outright foreign aid opponents a field day and contributes to the program's increasingly agonizing course through Congress. For instance, Representative Otto Passman, chairman of the House Appropriations Subcommittee on Foreign Operations and the *bête noire* of AID, took more than a little delight in calling attention to the solar-powered boat deal in debate on the fiscal 1963 foreign aid bill. "Of all the stupid waste of money that we have ever heard of and investigated during the years, I think we have unearthed the utmost in impractical projects of the never-never land."

The powerful Passman, a dapper Democrat from Louisiana's Fifth District, has almost singlehandedly slashed billions from foreign aid budget requests since he became chairman of the subcommittee in 1955. The full appropriations committee has a record of going along with him, and the House only rarely restores items to the pared-down budgets he brings to the floor. But Passman is against foreign aid "in principle." He even voted against the Marshall Plan.

It is the custom of Presidents and the bleeders among liberal politicians and journalists to sneer at Otto Passman, but to some extent this is because of an acute awareness of Passman's indefatigable research into the foreign aid program, which makes him a man who too often knows what he is talking about. Passman can take the taxpayer by the hand and personally escort him on tours of Far Eastern jungles and African veldts where his money has been thrown away by inept administrators of our international charities. No example of waste is too small for Passman to note and convert into a headline, and despite the sneers there is the awkward knowledge on Capitol Hill and in Foggy Bottom and at 1600 Pennsylvania Avenue that Passman has facts and figures with which to back up his strident complaints. Any day of the week, Passman can toss on his desk for inspection by a visiting reporter several hundred pounds of bulging files citing chapter and verse on foreign aid waste.

President Eisenhower once gave orders that Passman was never again to be invited to the White House, an edict that brought a cackle from the old-shoe Louisianan. "He needs me more than I need him," said Passman. And he was right, because from his powerful position in the House's money department Passman can manage a multimillion-dollar reduction in foreign aid appropriations merely by consulting his notebook and announcing that as a result of American economic succor to foreign lands alien steel has intruded on our ports at prices as much as $33 a ton less than the United States domestic price.

Passman always has a solid core of the anti-internationalist set ready to go along with him. But his patient, plodding labors in pursuit of those statistics that "prove" foreign aid is a "sheer giveaway," marked by appalling waste, have been winning him new support among those Congressmen more cordial to the foreign aid concept. Passman's efforts and the danger to the concept of continued perfunctory administration of America's aid program was dramatized by the ordeal of the fiscal 1964 AID budget.

The 1964 foreign aid budget got an epic mauling, not only from its traditional foes but from its erstwhile friends as well. Hardshell House members and Senate liberals alike gnawed it up one side and chewed it down the other. President Kennedy had launched it with a request for $4.9 billion, but, sensing the depth of an economy wave sweeping the Congress, pared it down to $4.5 billion.

The paring followed the Presidentially appointed Clay

committee report recommending a tightening of the foreign aid program. Appointment of the committee had undoubtedly been intended to mollify aid opponents and blunt the ax of the budget cutters. But the committee's report and the subsequent Administration decision to ask for $400 million less had quite the opposite effect. They left a taste of blood on the Congressional tongue.

The first half of the annual aid battle is the authorization process. This sets a ceiling on the amount of money Congress will give the Administration. The House cut the Administration's $4.5-billion request by an even billion to $3.5 billion. The Senate, traditionally more amenable to Presidential persuasion, put some of it back. The Foreign Relations Committee had reported out a $4.2-billion bill, but under bitter and sustained Senate floor attack led by Democratic Senator Wayne Morse of Oregon and others, the figure fell to $3.7 billion. A Senate-House compromise left it at $3.6 billion.

The second half of the annual fray is appropriation of the money. And it is in this round that Passman, as chairman of the House aid-money subcommittee, wields the big whip. He wielded it with his accustomed vigor—despite the famed "Johnson treatment."

President Lyndon Baines Johnson had, mere weeks before, taken over the reins of executive power. Because the aid program had been a highly significant tool in the Presidential exercise of foreign policy, this bill represented Johnson's first immediate challenge from the Congress which he once had dominated as Senate Majority Leader.

Johnson called Passman to the White House, urging that the entire $3.6-billion authorization be appropriated. Passman listened politely, as he had to other Presidents, and returned to the House, where he slashed the bill by $800 million to $2.8 billion. It was the biggest dollar cut since 1952 and the biggest percentage cut in foreign aid history.

He took the bill to the House floor with apologies—not for having cut so deep, but for not having cut more. A cornpone humorist, Passman presented himself as an unwilling Santa Claus to 100 foreign nations. He won not only laughter but votes. Such was the budget-cutting temper of the House and Passman's control over the bill's fate, that Administration leaders, although they deplored the cuts as too deep, dared not launch a counteroffensive. They feared such a tactic might backfire, resulting in even deeper cuts rather than a restoration of funds.

Instead, they placed their hopes again in the Senate. Johnson again put his prestige on the line. "We cannot oppose the spread of Communism and promote the growth of freedom by giving speeches," he argued. "A policy of weakness and retreat—which any further reduction at the appropriation state would represent—cannot be justified by the needs of our security, the financial strength of our nation or the attitude of our citizens."

The Senate responded, but lamely. It passed a $3.27 billion bill. And the eventual Senate-House compromise was pared to an even $3 billion in aid money—an amount almost $2 billion under the original $4.9 billion asked.

The sharply pared bill was not, however, without its victories. Eventually stricken from the compromise bill was a provision to ban Export-Import Bank underwriting of private credit sales to Communist countries. The House had twice insisted on this prohibition following a Soviet proposal to buy United States wheat. Congressional conservatives argued the wheat deal would leave Uncle Sam holding the bag.

President Johnson called the proposed wheat sales "good for our farmers and exporters, good for our shipping and railroad industry, good for our balance of payments, and good for the country." But his more urgent reason for insisting on removal of the ban on loan guarantees was basically political. He feared the Congressionally imposed ban would convince Khrushchev and other world leaders that the new United States President was a weakling easily overruled by Congress.

A White House memorandum revealed Johnson's awareness that allies anxiously watched the transition from Kennedy to Johnson Administrations, "to determine whether [Johnson] is strong enough to be a reliable leader of liberty or whether he is weak and they should base their policies on some calculation other than the strength of the United States." The memorandum noted also that "the countries of the Communist world are watching anxiously to determine whether the new President is so strong they will have to come to terms with him, or so weak that they can start hacking away at the Free World with impunity."

Another Administration victory salvaged from the badly mauled aid bills was restoration of the President's authority to grant "most favored nation" trade treatment to Communist Poland and Yugoslavia. This policy permits imports from a given country to enter the United States at the same low tariff rate as the most favored Free World nation. The preceding Congress had directed the President to eliminate liberal trade terms for Communist-controlled countries, although President Kennedy had not, in fact, yet done so for Poland and Yugoslavia. Opponents argued that the liberal trade policy only strengthened Communist regimes in the two countries. Proponents argued it was a valuable tool for loosening these countries' ties with Moscow and bringing them closer to the West.

But the fact was that it was December 30, 1963, six months after the 1964 fiscal year had begun, the last day of the long first session of the 88th Congress and little more than a week before the second session was to begin, that the foreign aid money bill was ready for Presidential signature.

By any standard it was a rout, and President Johnson knew it. He did what comes naturally to a Chief Executive confronted with a foreign aid crisis. He appointed another study committee—the ninth in fourteen years—to help carry out his pledge to Congress to submit a fiscal 1965 aid program that would be "more effective, efficient."

The new eight-man committee was composed of representatives of State, Defense and Treasury departments, the White House, the Peace Corps and AID Administrator David E. Bell himself. The President wanted its report by mid-January 1965, a fact that provoked skepticism both within and outside of Congress. Some leading aid sympathizers, like liberal Republican Senator John Sherman Cooper of Kentucky, a former Ambassador to India, thought only a more detailed and intensive study would answer the increasingly insistent demands for reassurance that our aid expenditures were productive.

On December 27, 1963, the Associated Press reported that the new committee was considering at least four proposals for splitting the program up: putting all AID operations for Latin America under a single head; giving lending operations of AID to one or more international agencies; setting up a special technical assistance agency; giving responsibility for military assistance exclusively to the Defense Department.

Any such "solution" to our aid program could only compound the problem which the creation of the Agency for International Development two years earlier had been designed to correct. By coordinating the entire foreign aid effort under one command, it was intended that meaningful execution, interpretation and evaluation of the program should result.

It was a good idea, and if it failed to endear the program to Congress, the fault lay not with the idea but with its execution. The program's problems stemmed, rather, from an apparent lack of consistent administration and want of candor with Congress and the people who pay for the aid program—the taxpayers—about how much was being spent, where, and what for.

The basic need was not for another reorganization. It was for a consistent policy, carefully administered and clearly explained, of putting our aid money for whatever purpose— military or economic—where it would demonstrably do the United States the most good. And, the efforts of the new committee notwithstanding, some Congressional aid backers foresaw only storm warnings ahead for the program.

There was no mystery as to why the liberals had revolted, and why a Democratic Congress had so treated a Democratic President and his steward, David Bell, the ablest director in foreign aid's history. The reasons were numerous but, more important, they were cumulative in character. Men like Senators Frank Church of Idaho, Albert Gore of Tennessee, Ernest Gruening of Alaska and Wayne Morse of Oregon—all Democratic liberals—were fed up with the apparent inability of any administration ever to bring any foreign aid program to an end. As Church pointed out in a terse, cogent essay for United Press-International, the list of recipient countries by 1963 had grown to 109, leaving only eight countries in the whole of the free world which were not getting some form of American subsidy. Even the rich, fully recovered nations of Western Europe and Japan were still receiving sizable grants of Uncle Sam's military equipment and supplies.

There was also the frustration suffered in efforts to shift foreign aid from gifts to loans. As Church pointed out, the United States would not have had so serious a problem with its balance-of-payments deficit had it loaned, instead of given, most of the money under the Marshall Plan to the countries of Western Europe. By 1963, we would have been calling back from the prosperous European countries, without hardship to them, the money we should have loaned them in the postwar years.

To be sure, the United States had established several years previously the Development Loan Fund, designed to place aid for economic development on a genuine loan, rather than grant, basis. But the flexibility permitted the DLF resulted in virtually all "loans" being made on forty-year repayment schedules, with generous grace periods during which no repayment of principal occurred, and with interest rates as low as .75 per cent. "In short," grumbled Church, "instead of giving away money and calling it a gift, we are now giving away money and calling it a loan. Even the Soviet Union, while denouncing the 'Wall Street Money-Changers,' never gets less than two per cent on long-term credits."

These men, long-time supporters of foreign aid, were also concerned by the sheer size of the program. Despite the billions poured into costly "impact" projects, they were discovering that outside of industrial Europe Uncle Sam's most conspicuous successes have been achieved through the least costly parts of the program—the Peace Corps, technical assistance, and surplus food. Church, Gore, et al demanded that the bigger projects be financed through greater use of international lending institutions such as the World Bank. These institutions, it was pointed out, could impose requirements necessary for sound investment management which are difficult for one sovereign nation to demand of another. Such a switch, of course, would also spread the burden, since the investment capital of the World Bank and others of its type is contributed by the wealthy industrial countries.

Even with these improvements, however, the liberals were demanding fundamental changes in the program—and threatening to withhold future support unless they were made. In particular, they looked with leery eye on the military assistance program, which had become both wasteful and exces-

sive. Vast quantities of arms had been handed over to countries wholly unable to use or maintain them. Military aid, it
was clear, should not have been started in Africa or continued
in Latin America, areas which are remote from either Russia
or Red China and where money is desperately needed for
public health, education and economic development.

Ten years after the fighting had ceased in Korea, the
United States was still keeping two American divisions there
at a cost of almost $500 million a year. Yet, after the outpour-
ing of American money, equipment, arms and training there
was still fear the South Koreans remained unable to guard
their narrow frontier. Every year, the United States had
poured $250 million into Formosa, indulging the dreams of
an old man named Chiang Kai-shek, who demanded an army
twice as big as necessary to defend his island and not a tenth
big enough to successfully invade the Red Chinese mainland.

More devastating comment on foreign aid came from
Senator Gruening, who made a one-man study of the program in ten Middle Eastern and African countries in 1962
and 1963. In recommending ten criteria to judge whether a
country should receive aid, Gruening declared that the program had been cheapened in the eyes of the world because
the United States had not insisted that the nations receiving
our assistance carry out programs of reform. He noted that
there were "at least twenty-two separate spigots" from which
United States aid flowed into foreign countries, and asked
that "these spigots be consolidated so as to preclude the
practice of foreign governments of shopping for funds from
spigot to spigot."

As others had done before him, Gruening pointed out the
Alice-in-Wonderland aspect of our so-called "loans." On such
loans made at .75 per cent interest for 40 years, it was as
though we gave the recipient country a grant of 50 to 75

per cent extra, since the United States had to pay about 4 per cent a year to borrow the money to make the loan.

Gruening and others also were concerned about the situation involving loans repayable in local currencies. Those currencies in turn were, as a rule, loaned back to the country for economic development, and because the loans are repayable with interest, the fund of local currencies available was constantly increasing. In Israel, for example, our AID program was at an end and the AID mission had been withdrawn. But during the next ten years, the American Embassy in Israel would be called upon to negotiate new loans in Israeli pounds amounting to $250 million, although our total AID program to Israel in the ten years from 1953 to 1962 was only $392 million. It also was a "disturbing thought" to Gruening that in the year 2003 the American Embassy in Athens would still be passing on local applications from the Greek government.

And, he asked, "Will not the interference of the United States in the local economic development of a nation be resented so long after the original loan has been made and when we are loaning not dollars but local currencies?" Gruening feared the United States "will never be able to get off the treadmill and that foreign aid will never be able to end in any country" unless Congress laid down some ground rules as to how local currencies should be spent in the future. He suggested renegotiating the loan agreements by offering substantial inducements for repayment in dollars, and/or the establishment of educational trust funds in those countries where the AID program was at an end and loans repayable in local currencies were outstanding.

Men like Gruening squirmed at the contradictions spawned in assorted bureaucratic snake pits. The United States was handing out $224 million a year to Egypt at a time when Egypt was spending $150 million a year in a war of aggression in Yemen, thus putting Uncle Sam in the position of financing Egypt's war. Moreover, since Jordan had been forced by Egypt's aggression to increase its armaments, and since the United States was furnishing economic aid to Jordan, the American taxpayer was also financing the efforts of at least one of Egypt's enemies.

Gruening's set of criteria was sound and made sense, which in Washington threatened it with the oblivion of the wastebasket. But it was valuable at least for showing a growing awareness in Congress of the foreign aid program's weaknesses. Here are Senator Gruening's criteria:

1. There is a reliable, stable, and reasonably efficient system of government and a basic cadre of trained and experienced public administrators;

2. There is a force of trained managerial personnel to administer intelligently any aided economic developments;

3. There is a genuine desire for economic development, a realization of the obligations entailed in such economic development, and a readiness to sacrifice in the present for future economic growth;

4. The budget of the country is austere and its income is not being spent on frills or on the import of luxury goods;

5. The laborers in factory and in field—the skilled and unskilled workers and farmers—will receive a just share of the benefits accruing from economic development;

6. There is no "flight" of private capital from the country;

7. The country is not engaged in unprovoked military attack on its neighbors or in an unnecessary arms buildup for that purpose;

8. The country is not committed to an economic system dedicated to the ultimate liquidation of private enterprise and investment;

9. There has been formulated a well-conceived, not overambitious, long-range economic development plan; and

10. Needed equitable tax and land reforms have been adopted or are in the process of adoption.

Such criteria, and the constructive criticisms of Congress' liberal bloc, had come too late to make complete sense out of the billions of dollars of taxpayers' money lavished on the free world since World War II. But there was hope that, since foreign aid remained a fact of Uncle Sam's international life, such proddings might bring about a rejuvenation of the program. If the White House, the State Department and the Pentagon took heed of the handwriting on the wall, perhaps there would be no more major frustrations and senseless spending of millions such as beset our campaign of enlightened self-interest in countries like South Vietnam.

4 *Uncle Santa in Vietnam*

The lead story in the *New York Times* of Sunday, August 25, 1963, was datelined Saigon, South Vietnam, and said in part:

Informed Vietnamese sources are bluntly warning Americans that the future of the anti-Communist cause is threatened because the Vietnamese public is losing confidence in the United States and is turning against the Americans.

Public bitterness toward the Saigon Government, it is said, is rapidly reaching out to the Americans. The Vietnamese say the bitterness has grown so strong that the anti-Communist cause is rapidly receding in the eyes of the public.

Vietnamese observers have told the Americans that even the relatively sophisticated elements of the population rarely have been more receptive to Communist propaganda than now. . . .

From 1955 through 1963 the United States had poured some $3 billion in economic and military assistance into the republic of South Vietnam. The *New York Times* story reflected the worst kind of waste in our foreign aid program; that is, not only failing to achieve in full measure the goal toward which we had lavishly spent, but alienating real or potential friends in the process. It was waste spawned by

63

faulty diplomacy. And the fault was compounded by the fact that South Vietnam since its birth in 1954 had been the keystone of our policy in Southeast Asia, where a group of small states, most of which had formerly been ruled by colonial regimes, lay within claw's reach of the Red Chinese Dragon.

The Vietnam incident stemmed from widespread internal dissatisfaction with the regime of Ngo Dinh Diem, who had been "our boy" and President of the republic since its establishment. Our involvement with Diem and the whole of Southeast Asia, an area of only casual concern to us before the Korean War, had stemmed from a massive shift in the power balance. The Korean War had served notice of Red China's imperial ambitions in the northern part of the Asian continent. The view southward was not encouraging. For while the Red Chinese empire was waxing bolder, our Western allies were withdrawing from, or being forcibly relieved of, their political responsibilities in Southeast Asia, leaving in their wake generally unstable, inexperienced and weak new nations. As they backed out, we backed in to fill the political vacuum that the Communists would have preferred to fill.

So it was that we became involved in South Vietnam, a fledgling nation somewhat smaller than Oklahoma with a population of 15,000,000. Our involvement actually began while it was still a part of French Indochina and presided over by the French puppet Emperor Bao Dai. After the outbreak of the Indochina war, we pumped some $1.2 billion into the country to prevent its being taken over by the Communist Viet Minh "Army of Liberation." Then came the 1954 military disaster at the French outpost of Dienbienphu which fell, after a gallant defense, to the Viet Minh.

The politically influential Diem was at this time in exile in the United States. He was anti-Communist and had once been held a Communist prisoner. He was also anti-colonialist and had left politics before World War II rather than work with the French. He wanted nothing less than Vietnamese independence. After the Dienbienphu disaster the desperate French met his demands and called him back to try to rally his people and salvage what he could from the Communists.

But two weeks after Diem was installed in Saigon as Premier, the French signed an accord in Geneva that halted the war and split the country in half at the 17th parallel. The more industrial North was to be Communist-controlled. The South, including Saigon and the rice-rich Mekong River delta, was to be non-Communist. France's influence in South Vietnam continued after the Geneva accord, but mostly in the fields of commerce, investment and culture. The United States was left to bolster the government in the areas that counted most—internal stability, economic support, and defense.

Along with this responsibility we inherited Diem, who, in turn, inherited a feeble and corrupt government lacking even the executive or administrative machinery to run it. The Army was controlled by a French puppet general who kept threatening to overthrow Diem. The notorious Binh Xuyen river pirates were in control of police and security forces, a concession they had bought from Emperor Bao Dai. The Cao Dai and the Hoa Hao, two religious sects, roamed the countryside with their own heavily armed private armies. And almost from its birth South Vietnam had been plagued by the Communist guerrillas—the Viet Cong.

The new republic in 1955 had rejected the Emperor and elected Diem to the Presidency. And, to his credit, he used a comparative lull in the Viet Cong guerrilla warfare between 1955 and 1959 to tidy up the country. Land reform boosted agricultural output. Education and social services were expanded. Some industrialization was begun. Communications were reopened and enlarged. And governmental authority was established to the extent that travel outside the major cities once again became safe.

In 1959, however, the guerrilla activity intensified. Night attacks a few miles from the capital were common, and within the capital itself there were bomb explosions. The Communists, some 10,000 of whom had blended back into South Vietnam's peasant landscape after the 1954 cease-fire, had grown to a primitively armed force of some 125,000, most of whom were irregulars. And despite our supply of modern equipment to the republic's 200,000-man regular military establishment and 170,000 irregulars, the situation worsened until by 1961 the government was near collapse.

Both Diem's government and the United States, calling in political, military and economic specialists, took a new hard look at the situation. The result was a decision to 1) intensify United States aid, 2) try to win non-Vietnamese mountain tribes to the republic's side, training and equipping them for defense against the Viet Cong, and 3) regroup the country's rural population into strategic hamlets in which they could collectively defend themselves against Viet Cong incursions. These hamlets would also serve as centers through which United States aid could be funneled to the rural populace. Acting on this plan, the United States by 1963 had some 14,000 tough, hard-nosed "military advisers" in Vietnam. The Viet Cong found them fair target, too. Some 100 Americans lost their lives.

By mid-1963 the plan seemed to be making headway. But to many dispassionate observers it had been apparent for some time that our substantial investment of military and economic aid in South Vietnam would not be enough to secure this "bastion" in Southeast Asia. At the request of President Kennedy, Senate Majority Leader Mike Mansfield of Montana in the fall of 1962 had headed a four-senator study mission into the area. They reported to the President:

"Even to give an initial military victory meaning will require a massive job of social engineering. . . . Practices of political organization which have been relied on most heavily to date in South Vietnam are, in many respects, authoritarian. While the plans for the strategic hamlets are cast in a democratic mold, it is by no means certain at this point how they shall evolve in practice. The evolution of the practices of the Central Government, to date, are not reassuring in this connection. . . .

"It is most disturbing to find that after seven years of the Republic, South Vietnam appears less, not more, stable than it was at the outset. It appears more removed from, rather than closer to, the achievement of popularly responsible and responsive government. The pressures of the Viet Cong guerrillas do not entirely explain this situation. In retrospect, the Government of Vietnam and our policies, particularly in the design and administration of aid, must bear a substantial, a very substantial share of the responsibility."

Stated more bluntly, the United States had for seven years been propping up a largely unloved authoritarian regime. While we were helping Diem's troops win over Communist guerrillas in the jungles and rice paddies, Diem in Saigon was losing the battle for the minds and hearts of his people. In this losing battle Diem also had help—an aristocratic and ambitious family. The government had become practically a family enterprise of which Diem had lost effective control. It was a militantly Catholic family in a predominantly Buddhist country. Diem's oldest brother, Ngo Dinh Thuc, Roman Catholic archbishop of Hué, controlled large amounts of church property and placed favorites in Diem's Cabinet. Ngo Dinh Can ran the city of Hué. Ngo Dinh Luyen had served as South Vietnam's Ambassador to Great Britain and several European countries.

But the most sinister influence was brother Ngo Dinh Nhu and Nhu's beautiful, wasp-waisted, acid-tongued, domineering wife. Nhu was Diem's political counselor, head of both the secret police and a 70,000-member Revolutionary Labor party. Madame Nhu bossed not only her Presidential brother-in-law but everyone else, high or low, military or civilian, within earshot. Converted to Catholicism with her marriage, she became a puritanical feminist and a national scold. Elected to the National Assembly in 1956, she rammed through legislation to outlaw prostitution, abortion, contraceptives, organized animal fights and taxi dancing.

Informed sources in Saigon agreed that the Nhus were behind the incident which the *New York Times* described as having undercut both American prestige and the cause of anti-Communism. It was a brutal crackdown on the Buddhists. Repression of the Buddhist majority by the Catholic Diem regime had long been a source of popular resentment. It also embarrassed the United States and the Vatican. The Buddhist priest class had become the repository of all Vietnamese dissatisfaction with Diem and his autocratic, suspicious and ruthless family.

When these dissatisfactions were dramatized by a Buddhist monk, Quang Duc, who burned himself to death in gasoline-soaked robes, Madame Nhu shrilled that the Buddhists had "barbecued one of their own monks, whom they intoxicated. And even that burning was not done with self-sufficient means, because they used imported gasoline."

The Diem regime's position was that the Buddhist monks were "Reds in yellow robes." After the recall of United States Ambassador Frederick E. Nolting the regime moved swiftly and brutally, in violation of pledges to the United States of religious tolerance. Buddhist monks and nuns were roughed up and arrested. Pagodas were burned.

Popular resentment rose to such a pitch that many of the

Vietnamese soldiers we had equipped and trained to fight Communists were returned to the capital to keep civil order. The Nhus obviously wanted to get this unpleasantness mopped up before the new and tougher United States Ambassador, Henry Cabot Lodge, arrived. It was charged Ambassador Nolting had been "soft" on the Diem regime, more eager to defend it than to concede and cope with the rising tide of popular Vietnamese dissatisfaction with it. By the time Lodge arrived, tough but late, our more than $4 billion investment in South Vietnam had been put in jeopardy. If popular sentiment throughout Buddhist Asia could be translated into dollars, our long identification with and support of Diem and his family-run police state had cost us untold millions.

The Communists, of course, were elated. Communist China, which had brutally suppressed Buddhism during its take-over in Tibet a decade earlier, seized the chance to divert and direct Buddhist attention to what it called the "United States-Diem" regime. Communist Dictator Mao Tse-tung from Peking urged South Vietnamese Buddhists to support the Communist guerrillas. Ho Chi Minh, President of Communist North Vietnam, quickly accused both the United States and Diem of religious persecution. Worldwide protest welled forth, and the United States was left with the gratuitous task of trying to demonstrate to the world that it did not hate Buddhists.

This is not to overstate the case. Conduct of the government had obviously been the responsibility of the Vietnamese. Contrary to Communist charges, we did not "run the government" of South Vietnam. But unquestionably our billions had kept it running. Tighter administration of our aid and more hardheaded diplomacy would have seen to it that our investment was not so seriously threatened.

The soft line with the Diem regime had not originated

with Ambassador Nolting. It was a policy of long standing. This was discovered by Albert M. Colegrove, a staff writer for Scripps-Howard Newspapers, who visited South Vietnam in the summer of 1959. In a no-holds-barred series of stories, Colegrove reported:

The byword of most high officials here is: "Keep your mouth shut, smile and don't rock the boat." . . .
Following a gutless, foolish made-in-Washington policy of "non-interference," we've forked over bundles of American cash to the fledgling, inexperienced Vietnam government, and then looked piously at the ceiling while the money melted away. Similarly, we've looked the other way while the Vietnamese government has set up an iron dictatorship that tolerates no criticism—a state now complete with recently created special military courts which can arrest, try, and condemn to death civilians in three days' time.
Practically everyone agrees that Free Vietnam, with 615 million Chinese and North Vietnamese Communists at her door, and with organized Red guerrillas within her borders, wouldn't last 10 days if she had an easy-going, American-style democracy. But must America put an official stamp of approval on police state methods?

Among frustrated, would-be boat rockers assigned to the South Vietnamese Mission one was quoted by Colegrove as saying, "You learn quickly. If you start criticizing the status quo, even mildly, you're gently warned your boss may consider you a trouble-maker, and might so state when he writes up your next efficiency report. This could louse up your career permanently. If you fail to take the hint and persist in crusading, they'll find a way to ship you out of here with no fuss, no muss. They shy away from firing you outright because that might spark off an investigation. But a year's leave—without pay—can be arranged."
The State Department tried to discredit Colegrove's re-

ports during Senate hearings. The Senate Foreign Relations Committee sent its own party over for a look. In the party was Democratic Senator Albert Gore of Tennessee, who first came to Congress from the district formerly represented by the great internationalist, Cordell Hull. Gore is in the Hull tradition. But he wound up supporting Colegrove's findings. "The conviction that [trade and aid] policies are necessary seems to me inescapable from a careful review of world conditions," Gore said. "This is all the more reason, however, why our programs should be clean and effective."

Gore was "disturbed by the growing authoritarian policies" of Diem, criticized the high cost of maintaining native military forces, and found that "United States policies in Vietnam have been characterized by loose, uncoordinated administration, sometimes within the country team itself and sometimes between Washington and the country team." The "major shortcoming," Gore reported, was failure of the United States to demand audits of Vietnamese use of our counterpart funds and the failure of the Vietnamese to make them.

But if aid administrators were slow about keeping track of our expenditures, they were Johnny-on-the-spot in planning for new outlays. A General Accounting Office investigation showed, for instance, that the aid agency had asked Congress to appropriate for fiscal year 1961 more than $5 million in equipment for Vietnam's Civil Guard, despite an already bulging "pipeline"—funds already available but not yet spent for this purpose.

GAO reported that our aid agency "considered it desirable to have these funds ready for obligation as soon as an agreement could be reached with Vietnam . . . because of the importance attached to the project from the viewpoint of promoting political stability and internal security. . . ."

Aid administrators, the report continues, "anticipated that about $2 million of the funds obligated through fiscal year

1960 would remain unsubobligated—that is, not earmarked for specific commodities, because of technical considerations in regard to procurement and installation of communications and other special equipment. . . .

"Considering the large amount of prior years funds in the pipeline and the various conditions delaying prompt procurement action, we [the GAO] believe that the 1961 funding request for commodities was not realistic."

For those readers who may have become discombobulated by such bureaucratic jargon as "unsubobligated," the report meant simply that the GAO thought the aid agency was padding its expense account.

In Vietnam we had also been neglecting the simpler economies. A team of House Foreign Operations Subcommittee investigators reported in 1962 that we were spending more to recap military tires for the Vietnamese in Saigon than it would have cost us to buy new tires in the United States. This nonsensical arrangement was the result of a "political compromise" with the Diem regime on the official rate of exchange. The local currency, the piaster, had been assigned an official exchange rate of 35 to the dollar. The United States had approved this rate even though an expert we had hired to explore the situation had recommended a rate of 80 piasters to the dollar. Thus it was that we were spending in United States-supplied local currency $10.24 to recap a 600-by-16 tire that could have been bought new in the United States for $9.50. The recapping job on a 750-by-20 tire was costing $22.40. Bought new in the United States, the tire then cost $19.10.

Said the investigators, "The United States could have greater assurance that its economic aid would be more effective if it insisted that a sound foreign exchange rate should be a prerequisite of any program of economic development. In both Turkey and Korea realistic exchange rates have been established in accordance with United States policy. If the United States could exercise the same degree of supervision and control over the use of our aid in all countries as it does in a few and could enforce the same standards of austerity, our foreign aid operations would be more economical and effective."

In their investigations the House team also found that Uncle Sam had wasted $300,000 in the procurement of trucks for the Vietnam Civil Guard to use in anti-guerrilla warfare. This came about because our economic left hand apparently did not know what our military right hand was doing. The responsibility for bankrolling the Civil Guard, a sort of state police force, was transferred from our military to our economic aid program in the spring of 1961. Our military aid group in Vietnam decided that 260 trucks were badly needed for the Guard and asked the economic people to order them since they had money available. The economic people ordered United States commercial vehicles.

The House investigators in a meeting with the Economic and Military Mission people and the United States Ambassador said in effect, "Look, fellows, the Army at this very moment is contracting to have comparable trucks for our military aid program produced in Japan. You can buy them $1,100 apiece cheaper there, if the trucks are available. We'll check this out for you when we get back to Washington."

If anybody had thought of this before, they had not thought about it very much. Eight days after the House probers left South Vietnam, the military group cabled the Pacific Commander in Chief saying that the order for commercial trucks had been based on an assumption that the military trucks could not be supplied. Two days after that— and before the military people had got a reply to their cable —the economic people signed the contract for the commercial trucks. And eleven days after the signing, the military people got a cable replying, sure, we've got lots of trucks available in Japan. But by that time it would have cost $175,000 more than the savings involved to cancel the commercial contract.

Concluded the investigators, "It is clear that two agencies were dealing with each other at arm's length, neither having possession of all the facts, with the result that the United States is paying nearly $300,000 more for the trucks than was necessary." There was, however, a modestly silvered lining to this episode. At the same time it was considering the truck purchase, the American aid group in Vietnam was also considering the purchase of 522 jeeps from commercial sources. It turned out that our Army-contract operation in Japan also had a bumper crop of jeeps on hand. Thanks to the House investigators, the savings amounted to $150,000.

There were other oddities uncovered. In this strategic hot spot our aid had financed some $11 million worth of civilian passenger cars between 1954 and 1958. We never did this in Korea. Obviously the passenger cars were going to Saigon, the "Paris of the Orient," and other Vietnamese cities. Noted the House survey team, "One of the important characteristics of life in Vietnam is the contrast between life in Saigon and other cities and life in the country. In addition to the differences in comfort and opportunities for amusement, there is the fact that cities are, in general, secure from Communist violence while country dwellers live in constant danger of extortion and assassination.

"To the extent that economic assistance is continued on a 'business as usual' basis except for less emphasis on the country and more on the city . . . the linkage of the rural population to the Government of Vietnam is weakened."

Colegrove's earlier findings had also indicated a preoccupation with comfortable Saigon living by a well-paid and "clubby" gaggle of our aid experts, who found it pleasanter to do unbusinesslike business with the urbane Ngo family than to undertake the more arduous task of getting our aid dollars meaningfully used among the Communist-harried peasantry. The prevailing attitude was typified by a $1,160-a-month-plus-free-rent United States press information officer who advised Colegrove against a fact-finding trip into the countryside.

"You can get the whole picture in Saigon," the taxpayer-paid press agent said. "No sense tramping around out there in the boondocks. Terribly hot and dirty, you know, and you can't get much from the peasants except disease. All the key people are here."

This attitude had resulted in the use of our tax dollars to satisfy Madame Nhu's insistence that President Diem's official toilet be soundproofed to forestall embarrassment while he was broadcasting from his office. But it obviously had not convinced the growing proportion of the impoverished Vietnamese citizenry that either Diem or Uncle Sam was necessarily good for them. Popular dissatisfaction, climaxed by the overthrow of Diem, substantiated the point apparent to Colegrove four years earlier.

Findings that American aid had been abused and subverted by the Diem regime were supported by none other than "Dragon Lady" Nhu's own father, Tran Van Chuong, former South Vietnamese Ambassador to the United States, who resigned in protest after the 1963 Buddhist incidents. Diem and his family had "become the strongest roadblock to victory because they have misused American aid to suppress their own people instead of using the aid to unite the people in the fight against the Communists," the former Ambassador charged.

Chuong said his son-in-law Nhu was to President Diem "what Hitler was to President Hindenburg, with the difference that Hindenburg knew it and President Diem does not know it. . . . If I were an American citizen I would not vote for a mandatory aid cut to South Vietnam, but I would give the United States government the power to make such cuts, total or selective, as it deems necessary."

We finally did suspend commercial dollar aid after the raids on the Buddhist pagodas. These were dollars that had been used to finance imports, which were sold to licensed Vietnamese merchants for local currency at less than the free market rate of exchange. This currency, in turn, was used to finance the country's military budget. We also cut off aid to Nhu's troops. Thus, Nhu complained that the aid slow-down would ultimately have both military and economic impact on the country, and the *Times of Vietnam,* which often reflected the Nhu viewpoint, quoted an anonymous Vietnamese as asking, "Who is the United States fighting— us or the Communists?"

The United States was trying, in fact, to fight both. But it had become increasingly clear that the Communist guerrilla forces would never be subdued as long as the repressive Diem-Nhu regime was more interested in cementing its own control over the country than in battling the Viet Cong. Former Ambassador Chuong reported, for instance, that the nation's four army corps generals had "only an indirect and theoretical command of troops." The national Army's seven divisions, he said, were really commanded by colonels and lieutenant colonels who took orders from either Nhu or Diem. Meanwhile our own military personnel in South Viet- nam, charged with helping the Vietnamese press the war against the Viet Cong, were under attack from Madame Nhu. Our junior advisers, she said, were "little soldiers of fortune—immature, excited and adventurous young officers who always believe that they are magicians but who are only apprentices."

The situation invited explosion. It occurred on November 1, 1963—All Saints' Day—while Madame Nhu was on a visit to the United States to drum up public support for her family's regime. A military coup, rumored for months, was led by Lt. Gen. Duong Van Minh, forty-seven, a six-foot, 200-pound, French-trained veteran whom Diem had once embraced for putting the Binh Xuyen river bandits out of business. It was a comparatively bloodless coup that lasted less than twenty-four hours. But Diem and Nhu were among the casualties—murdered.

Despite the fact that the general, known as "Big Minh," and his junta suspended the constitution and dissolved the national assembly, they disclaimed any political ambitions and named Nguyen Ngoc Tho, Diem's figurehead vice-president since 1956 and a Buddhist, as Premier of their government.

Although the United States formally expressed its disapproval of the Diem-Nhu murders, it was quick to recognize the new government. For "Big Minh" pledged what we wanted most—a more vigorous pursuit of the guerrilla war—and at least stood a greater chance of winning popular support than the old Diem regime had. But only months later "Big Minh" himself was overthrown in still another bloodless coup headed by Major General Nguyen Khanh, who promptly proclaimed himself Prime Minister, Chairman of the Military Junta, Defense Minister and Chief of State. Khanh is reported to be a friend of the United States. Exactly what our relations with him will be remains to be seen, but for better or worse he has become our new—and only—hope for improvement. Had our policy with the Diem regime been firmer, had the aid cutoff come earlier, we could probably have saved some time, some money, and a bit of face in the face-conscious East.

5 The Expensive Mr. Sukarno

In one of the classic understatements of 1963, Seymour J. Janow, Assistant AID Administrator for the Far East, told Representative Otto Passman's Foreign Aid Appropriations Subcommittee, "Aid to Indonesia is clearly an issue of some public discussion in the United States."

Indeed it was. Public debate was loud and acid. Private discussions of our aid investment in the sprawling archipelago were salted with expletives, many of them used to describe the republic's saber-rattling, anti-Western President Sukarno. During Senate debate on the fiscal 1964 foreign aid authorization bill Democratic Senator Wayne Morse called him "one of the most corrupt men on the face of the earth— a trickster, invidious and clever."

Into Indonesia, composed of some 3,000 islands strewn across 3,000 square miles of ocean between Southeast Asia and Australia, we had through fiscal 1963 poured $804 million of economic aid and some $77 million in military assistance. Janow, in seeking approval of 1964 funds, presented the case for our aid investment this way:

"We have aid programs in Indonesia for two basic purposes: To help block the Communists' bid for their greatest

prize since China, by strengthening those Indonesian elements, institutions and conditions which will resist Communism internally . . . [and] to help focus Indonesia's energies
and great potential on the development of an independent, responsible nation.

"Indonesia is one of the world's largest countries, fifth in
population [nearly 100,000,000], and with resources capable
of making it a great power. It lies astride the main north-
south and east-west communications lines in Asia. Indonesia's
Communist party (PKI) is the largest outside the Communist bloc, by far the best organized party in Indonesia, but
President Sukarno and the Army have so far resisted pressure to give Communists key positions in government.

"The Communist bloc has made Indonesia its No. 1 target
of military and economic aid in the past three years—about
$1.7 billion in cumulative commitments of which three-
fourths were made in the past three years. Indonesia is not
now a Communist country, and should not be treated as such.
Indeed, its entry into the bloc would undermine and threaten
the entire Southeast Asian mainland."

Also, he went on, the aid totals we had given the republic
were misleading in that $169 million was bestowed while the
Dutch still controlled the country, $206 million was in Pub-
lic Law 480 surplus commodities, and $164 million was in
Export-Import Bank loans, on which the republic had repaid
$64.8 million. Fiscal 1963 aid to Indonesia included $38.1
million from the Agency for International Development and
$63 million in surpluses. The AID total included $17 million in loans. Actually, Janow argued, our aid to Indonesia
had been "very small in relation to the country's size and the
critical challenge we face there."

Possibly so. But Sukarno's performances were not of a
kind that encouraged openhandedness from the United
States. Passman just happened to have a couple of press

clippings at hand when AID Director Bell appeared before his subcommittee. One reported a banquet Red Chinese President Liu Shao-chi had given for Sukarno during a visit to Indonesia. Sukarno used the occasion to call Red China and Indonesia "the pillars of the new emerging forces" and predict that they would see the day when "the old established forces" (the West) would collapse.

Another story reported Sukarno's acceptance of a lifetime appointment as Chief of State by the 600-member People's Consultative Congress. The appointment was applauded by Communist party Chairman D. N. Aidit, who said, "Indonesian Communists are friends of Sukarno." Snapped Passman, "I'm just wondering if we could not find some friends to whom to give our money, instead of to that country."

There were, however, even more recent outrages to feed the animus of foreign aid opponents. Sukarno's satrapy, thanks to the economic ineptitude of its President, was financially in a state of near anarchy. One of the purposes of our aid was to stabilize the economy. To this end we had granted a $17 million "emergency" loan. Yet the same week we made the loan, Sukarno and Company announced they were going to spend $20 million to buy three plush United States jet airliners. Red-faced AID officials confessed they had not known about the proposed purchase. It was a contretemps made to order for "Otto the Terrible." Passman pounced. "Then," he said, "I would certainly discount substantially any justifications you [AID] people make for any type of loan to Indonesia, if you do not know any more about what is going on than that."

Summarized Republican Representative William E. Minshall of Ohio, "We got hoodwinked." Added Democratic Representative George W. Andrews of Alabama, "I do not think any country which can spend twenty million dollars for plush airplanes is in such dire financial straits that they

have to have an emergency loan from us." Explained Passman, "They are familiar with the gullibility of Uncle Sam."

A later incident, although in itself trivial, was symptomatic
of the irritations attendant upon playing Santa Claus to the
likes of Sukarno. We loaned him $8 million for a fine new
highway. Came dedication day, and Sukarno decreed that
no American flag could be flown at the ceremony. A red,
white and blue emblem of the Agency for International Development would be allowed next to the ceremonial ribbon.
But no American flag could be flown next to the eighty-eight
Indonesian flags displayed at the opening of the four-lane
divided highway on the outskirts of Indonesia's capital,
Jakarta. A United States Embassy staff member noted, "Certainly Indonesia is under no legal commitment to fly a foreign flag on its soil, but it is considered an international
diplomatic courtesy that on such occasions as this one . . .
both countries can fly their respective flags."

Passman and his posse of Indonesian critics had a point.
Passman usually did. He might not see the woods for the
trees, but he knew a sick tree when he saw one. The larger
woodsy-type prospect, however, was hardly more encouraging from the standpoint of the United States and her Western allies. Britain and the Netherlands were pulling out of
their long-held territories in Southeast Asia—and Sukarno
did nothing to ease their withdrawal pains. Malaysia was a
case in point.

The new British Commonwealth nation was conceived as
an anti-Communist bastion in Southeast Asia and was born
on September 16, 1963. It was composed of the independent
federation of Malaya, Singapore and the former crown colonies of North Borneo and Sarawak. It was the dream of Malaya's pro-Western Prime Minister, Tunku Abdul Rahman.
The eleven states of Malaya had been a British dependency
until August 21, 1957, when they achieved independence and

became a sovereign member of the Commonwealth. With the addition of the three former British territories to the new and larger federation, British colonialism was gone from Southeast Asia, except for the crown colony of Hong Kong.

Sukarno gave it a hot farewell. He turned mobs loose in Jakarta to sack British residences, burn the Embassy and the British Ambassador's car in protest of Malaysia's birth. The Malaysian Embassy was also attacked. Sukarno objected most to North Borneo's membership in the new federation. Indonesia controlled all the rest of the vast island. Along with Communist China, he saw in the new state a disguised "neo-colonial" power which, under treaty, permitted British troops to remain. Sukarno's Army chief boasted of the training of 6,000 anti-British, anti-federation guerrillas to operate on the island.

In retaliation, Malaysia broke off relations with Indonesia and with the Philippines, where demonstrations of somewhat lesser intensity had also occurred. (Philippine disaffection also stemmed from disputed claims to North Borneo.) The new nation was obviously off to a rocky start—and Sukarno had both the will and the wherewithal to keep up the pressure. The wherewithal was a disproportionately large and modern military machine, 80 per cent of which was Soviet-supplied. He had a standing army of 300,000. His sophisticated military hardware included a hundred Russian MIG jet fighters, a dozen MIG-21 long-range jets, twenty IL-28 intermediate and long-range jet bombers, ten TU-16 bombers armed with air-to-surface missiles and capable of ranging 5,000 miles. At sea he had six destroyers, four submarines, two fleet tankers and other equipment.

Some of Indonesia's war potential we ourselves had supplied. And there were charges that Sukarno was using our equipment to menace the new nation which we wished well. In the fall of 1963, for instance, Republican Representative

Oliver P. Bolton of Ohio blasted our State Department for approving the shipment of spare parts for ten Lockheed C-130 "Hercules" troop transports Indonesia had bought from us for $30 million in 1959. When Indonesia bought the planes it had "assured our State Department that they would not be used for aggressive military purposes," Bolton said. But since then, he charged, Sukarno had used the planes to drop paratroopers and supplies into the Malaysian North Borneo area. State replied it had no evidence the planes were being used for any "offensive" activity.

The basic fact is, however, that with one hand Sukarno had been accepting our predominantly "economic" assistance. With the other he had been bleeding the economy to build up a war machine. By late 1963 he was more than a billion dollars in debt to the Soviet Union for military hardware. Carrying charges alone on that debt came to more than $82 million a year.

Sukarno and Indonesia had come to prominence by the sword, and dashing, rabble-rousing Sukarno apparently saw it as the instrument of further growth. Indonesia, formerly known as the Netherlands East Indies, had been for more than three centuries under Dutch control, and was a Dutch colony at the outbreak of World War II. The Japanese in the early days of the war quickly took over and permitted some local self-government. Sukarno and another nationalist leader, Mohammed Hatta, were permitted to set up a national government in the closing days of the war. They proclaimed Indonesia's independence on August 17, 1945.

There followed four years of fighting the Dutch, after which sovereignty was transferred to a United States of Indonesia—led by Sukarno as its first President. Unrest within the new sixteen-state union led to the creation of a republic with Sukarno in even firmer control. In violation of earlier pledges, the new republic, with the support of the Indo-

nesian Communist party, expropriated some $1 billion in
Dutch property.

Under Sukarno, Indonesia also took over Belgian-owned
rubber and palm oil estates valued at $45 million, raised its
share of profits from foreign oil companies from 50 to 60 per
cent, and pressed its claim to Netherlands New Guinea,
which the Indonesians called Irian. Indonesian paratroopers
raided the territory. Finally, with United States-United Nations mediation, it was agreed that Indonesia would take it
over with the promise to conduct not later than 1969 a
plebiscite in which residents could choose between Indonesian annexation and full independence.

Sukarno encouraged and exploited the understandable
anti-colonial bias of his people to bolster his own popularity.
Although he was anti-West, there was also some evidence
that he was more pro-Sukarno than pro-Communist. He used
Communists in the lower echelons of his government, but
resisted their moves to take it over. He wanted co-equality
among religious, nationalist and Communist groups in the
government.

The Army was the chief hope of pro-Western forces within
Indonesia. But pro-Western Gen. Abdul H. Nasution, Chief
of Staff of the Indonesian Army Forces and Minister of Defense, warned, "If after five years this government fails in
economic progress, that may be the chance for the [Com-
munists] to take over." General Nasution was so quoted by
Jerry A. Rose in a November 2, 1963, *Saturday Evening Post*
article on Sukarno that concluded:

Sukarno obviously continues on his "international adventures."
Today there is Malaysia. Tomorrow, what next? Portuguese
Timor? Australian East New Guinea? Both are Sukarno's neighbors, and no doubt he covets them. But first comes Malaysia—
and Southeast Asia may soon erupt in chaos. And there will be
suffering for all, but particularly the Indonesians.

Indeed, Sukarno's adventures had already visited hardships on his people. He had sacrificed the domestic economy to his jingoist ambitions and flamboyant whims. "The nation is bankrupt, yet Sukarno purchased some 7,000 midget sport cars from Japan for luxury purposes," reported Senator William Proxmire of Wisconsin in blasting aid to Indonesia. "Sukarno has indicated his intention to make a fancy extension of the airport runway on Bali out over water at four or five times the conventional cost. Why? The reason we have from Sukarno himself. He believes that the Hong Kong airport is beautiful and wants one like it."

Sukarno, whom Proxmire described as a "new Oriental Hitler," collected other prestige trappings while his countrymen struggled merely to subsist. Thirteen million dollars in Japanese war reparations went into the fancy Hotel Indonesia, fourteen stories with a turquoise façade. A complex of four stadiums for his Asian Games cost $17 million and was called the "Glory of Bung [Brother] Karno."

Meanwhile Indonesia, once a major rice-producing area and exporter of rice, was forced to import a million tons a year. Once the world's major rubber supplier, she had fallen behind Malaya. Once a major producer of tin, her production had dropped about two-thirds over a period of fifteen years. Sugar production also fell. Retail prices rose—almost eight times in eight years. In 1962 the price of rice, a staple in the Indonesian diet, had climbed 17 per cent, eggs were up 139 per cent and sugar was up 239 per cent.

The combination of Sukarno's boycott of Malaysia, his troublemaking in North Borneo and his economic irresponsibility at home finally proved too much even for our State Department, which in the fall of 1963 suspended all new economic aid. Reservations about aid to Indonesia had earlier been expressed this way by the Clay committee:

"Because of its population, resources and geographic position, [Indonesia] is of special concern to the free world. However, we do not see how external assistance can be granted to this nation by free world countries unless it puts its internal house in order, provides fair treatment to foreign creditors and enterprises, and refrains from international adventures. If it follows this path, as we hope it will, it deserves the support of free world aid sources."

Among those who decided that Sukarno's Indonesia had not followed the prescribed path were both houses of the United States Congress. Both adopted amendments to the 1964 foreign aid authorization bill that would deny aid to Indonesia unless the President specifically found that it was in our national interest to do so. A measure of the intensity of feeling was a statement by liberal Republican Senator John Sherman Cooper of Kentucky, former Ambassador to India, who could be counted on for a sympathetic understanding of Asia's problems and considerable tolerance for their solution. Senator Cooper, nevertheless, supported the Proxmire amendment to ban aid to Indonesia with this observation:

"In past years, during the administration of President Eisenhower and the administration of President Kennedy, I opposed amendments which I thought would unduly restrict the President in what he would consider the proper conduct of foreign policy, and I have also opposed such amendments in connection with the foreign aid bill. . . . However, I wholeheartedly support this amendment. . . . Indonesia, which is very rich in resources, has been greatly mismanaged by the Sukarno government and . . . has also built up a very large and very expensive military machine which recently has been used aggressively . . . toward Malaysia. I believe our adoption of the amendment is entirely justified. I know there are good elements in the government of Indonesia, and I am sure the people of Indonesia are good and great. But it is my judgment that Sukarno is perhaps the most irresponsible leader of any government in the world today. So I hope the administration will not give Indonesia one penny of either loans or grants or any other form of aid."

In the course of his remarks Senator Cooper had put his finger on a central conflict between the executive and legislative branches over foreign aid. He spoke of "unduly" restricting Presidential conduct of foreign policy, which is the constitutionally assigned responsibility of the Chief Executive. To the extent that aid is a tool of foreign policy, Congressionally imposed restrictions on its use do limit the President's range of resources to deal with a particular problem at a particular time. Thus, after the Senate's adoption of the Indonesian ban, along with limitations on aid to Yugoslavia and Egypt, Secretary of State Dean Rusk at a press conference expressed his concern about Congress's tendency to "legislate foreign policy."

But Rusk's complaint that Congress was trying to snap the foreign aid purse shut merited only qualified sympathy. Congress has never been noted for penny-pinching—as any taxpayer who reads newspapers knows. The rash of Congressional parsimony was clearly caused by its conviction that the executive department had failed to drive meaningful bargains with the aid money Congress had provided over the years—a conviction that welded together a curious coalition of liberals and mossbacks who in chorus said, in effect, that they were sick of being short-changed.

Thus Proxmire, in arguing for the aid-to-Indonesia ban, reported, "We provided grants for the construction of a highway bypass outside Jakarta. This bypass was constructed very rapidly, with attendant waste, in order to permit transportation to the Soviet games. Yet the games were held in a Soviet-built stadium and we received no appreciation or thanks for the funds so used. . . . The United States government in Indonesia has purchased enough jeep spare parts to fill a large warehouse in Jakarta. The Indonesians now refuse to allow United States personnel into this warehouse, presumably because they are selling the spare parts. Similarly, a number of jeep station wagons were imported for use by AID field technicians, yet only four technicians have received their station wagons and the Indonesians refuse to turn over the remaining vehicles to AID. The same thing occurred with some Chevy II's, which were purchased for the chief of the AID malaria team. An Indonesian military colonel took two of the vehicles and released only one to AID."

In reply to Secretary Rusk's complaint Senator Morse reminded him that Congress, as the branch that votes aid money, has its own responsibilities. "We're not quitting foreign aid," Morse said. "We're trying to strengthen it." Morse, too, was correct. For it was in the mutual interest of both branches that the program remain at least comprehensible enough to the electorate so that a legislator could politically afford to vote for it.

An accretion of foreign aid fiascos had so weighted down the public's buoyant faith in the aid principle that some legislators—like Morse—warned that the good ship Foreign Aid was in danger of complete submersion. And Indonesia's Sukarno personified all the barnacles that had ever encrusted her hull. The Indonesian amendment, however, still left the President considerable freedom in negotiations with Sukarno. It amounted, in fact, to not much more than a Congressional statement of disapproval. The President could at any time resume aid grants or loans to Indonesia by finding it in our national interest and so advising the Congress.

This was a far cry from what some liberals—including Morse—wanted. Morse would have had the Congress stop the program cold by 1965 and start it up again under a new set of rules. Beneficiary nations would be halved—no more than fifty could get our aid and these would have to be nations where aid "really [could] do some good in strengthening freedom." Such countries would have to apply for aid "under the terms and conditions" we offered.

Morse probably expressed the anger and frustration of millions of Americans when in a Senate floor speech he lashed out at the September, 1963, "suspension" of aid to Sukarno. "Let us not be fooled," Morse said. "That is the 'slap on the wrist' stage, the calling of 'naughty, naughty' to Sukarno. But . . . it will not be long before he will make more false promises and unreliable statements; and the State Department will say, 'But we have no alternative; things will be worse if we do not help him.' But . . . what 'will be worse if we do not help' will be a lot of scarecrow fears that will be dragged up, and therefore he will receive more of our aid, and away we will go again with false starts and stops and stops and starts . . . instead of cutting off our aid at the pockets, and no longer dealing with Indonesia. . . .

"The old scarecrow argument, 'If we do not do something for them, the Commies will come in' . . . has cost the United States taxpayers hundreds of millions of dollars; and it is about time the American people say in answer to it, 'Why should we care? We have offered to support stability in Indonesia; we have offered to support a government which would recognize and respect human dignity and human rights, instead of tyranny and police state methods.' . . . I have sat in the Foreign Relations Committee for years and have heard that argument used under both Republican administrations and Democratic administrations; and I do not buy it any more . . . I really never find any significant change in the policies of the State Department from one party administration to another. . . .

"America is defended in that part of the world by the Seventh Fleet, American airpower, and American troops in the Pacific. . . . All of South Vietnam is not worth a single American boy. Neither is Indonesia. We do not need those parts of the world to defend American security in the Pacific. It is about time that we stopped pouring the American taxpayers' money into one rathole after another in that area of the world. If they want to go Communist, let them boil in Communist juices. Perhaps one of the greatest disservices that we could perform for Khrushchev would be to let him take over some of those countries. . . ."

Another aid critic—at the conservative end of the political spectrum—summed up with a homily another popular reaction to aid expenditures. Democratic Senator Herman Talmadge of Georgia asked Morse if he had ever heard the quotation: "If it costs a friend to make a dollar, keep the friend. If it costs a dollar to make a friend, keep the dollar." Replied Morse, "I certainly have. It is apropos of the whole foreign aid program."

It is hard altogether to agree with Talmadge and Morse on that. It is naïve to assume that what we had been trying to buy was abiding friendship—which, as the homily indicated, cannot be bought. We were trying to buy time, political advantage, create a present and future climate in Indonesia which would accommodate our legitimate interests in that part of the world. Had our aid investments been predicated over the years on their generation of unalloyed love for the United States, they should have been written off years ago. Rich uncles are less beloved than envied. But even rich uncles deserve a return on an honest investment—and the growing consensus was that in Sukarno's Indonesia Uncle Sam was getting gypped.

6 $450 Million Worth of Laos

Before leaving Southeast Asia it is imperative to look in on Laos, a remote and not very comic-opera little country, most of which is inaccessible jungle. It has only 2,500,000 people, most of whom live in scattered and primitive villages. And except for its immediate neighbors and France, most of the world had been blissfully unaware of its existence before it became independent in 1954. Like Cambodia and Vietnam, Laos had been part of French Indochina. It was historically known as the Land of a Million Elephants. We transformed it into the Land of Half a Billion Dollars. During the Indochina conflict we gave France some $30 million for use in Laos. Between 1955 and 1962 our aid to Laos came to $450 million—the equivalent of $180 for every man, woman and child. Considering the size and nature of the country, it was the most intensive aid effort we had undertaken anywhere in the world. A good deal of it was wasted.

Independence had transformed the sleepy little Buddhist kingdom on Red China's southern border into a cold-war battlefield. In 1953 the Laotian Army consisted of two battalions, totaling fewer than 1,000 men. Less than a decade later 100,000 Laotians were bearing arms as three major factions warred to determine whether democracy, communism or neutralism would direct the country's future. In 1953 the United States had only two officials in all of Laos. By 1961, the peak of our commitment, there were 850, and in the spring of that year the United States was seriously considering direct military intervention to preclude a take-over of the country by the Communists.

We were supporting the pro-Western government. Russia was airlifting arms to the pro-Communist Pathet Lao guerrilla group led by Prince Souphanouvong. A third faction was headed by Souphanouvong's half brother, Prince Souvanna Phouma, who had been independent Laos' first Prime Minister. This faction favored a neutralist policy and was sharply critical of United States aid to the Royal Laotian Army. In March of 1961 the Pathet Lao, aided by advisers and artillerymen from Communist North Vietnam, launched a major drive. They overwhelmed government troops in central Laos, forcing them to retreat southward. By April the Army, led by Gen. Phoumi Nosavan, had lost effective control of areas north of the country's administrative capital, Vientiane.

We conferred with our allies in the Southeast Asia Treaty Organization (SEATO). Thailand, Laos' worried neighbor, urged immediate SEATO military action. We supported this approach. France and Great Britain, however, urged negotiation and the return to office of neutralist Souvanna Phouma. Great Britain negotiated with Russia for the calling of an immediate cease-fire. Those two nations also asked India to convene the International Control Commission (composed of Indians, Canadians and Poles) and called for a fourteen-nation conference in Geneva to discuss Laos' future. We went along. On July 23, 1962—fourteen months after the conference had opened—the signatories pledged to respect Laos' neutrality.

They would not interfere in its internal affairs or use the territory to interfere in the internal affairs of Laos' neighbors, the signatories agreed. They also pledged to withdraw any military forces they had in the country. Meanwhile, the rival Laotian leaders had got together in Zurich to try to iron out their differences. They agreed to form a provisional government under King Savang Vathana. Neutralist Prince Souvanna Phouma was named Premier, but the leadership was shared with pro-Communist Prince Souphanouvong and pro-Western Gen. Phoumi Nosavan.

The Geneva accord resulted in withdrawal of our military aid Mission and a consequent reduction of aid expenditures from a peak of $73 million in 1962 to a 1963 level of about $40 million. Our economic aid, of course, continued. But one must hope that future gifts will prove to have been more prudently bestowed than many of our past financial favors. The watchdog House Foreign Operations Subcommittee turned up evidence of outrageous maladministration, conflict of interest and even bribery in our program in Laos.

They found, for instance, that we loaded Laos down with so much aid that we defeated some of our objectives in giving it. Independence found Laos with only the most rudimentary machinery for tax collection and the administration of government. Raising revenues was made more difficult because the economy was based in large measure on simple barter, rather than exchange of goods for money. So, as we had done in Vietnam, we took over from France practically the entire burden of financing the former French protectorate. But we pumped money into the simple Laotian economy so fast that it could not be absorbed. At one point the Laos government had a foreign exchange reserve of $40 million, or the equivalent of about a year's United States-financed aid. Between 1953 and 1958 the cost of living doubled. And speculators had a field day.

At the outset our major program had been military. We supported the entire military budget. The problem was to generate enough local currency to pay, maintain and house the 25,000-man Royal Laotian Army. Our usual method of generating local currency had been to finance an import program for the country aided. The sale of imported commodities would generate the local currency—in the case of Laos, the kip. But in the first several years 72 per cent of our aid to Laos was in the form of cash grants, and only 28 per cent in commodity imports. The ICA contended this device was used in the interest of time. The General Accounting Office reported that it was also used because the impoverished Laotian economy could not absorb enough imports to generate the necessary kips.

Related to this problem was the unrealistic official exchange rate of 35 kips to the dollar at a time when free markets in Bangkok, Hong Kong and elsewhere were offering an exchange as high as 110 to the dollar. This invited Laos merchants to speculate in foreign exchange without actually importing goods, or to import goods only to ship them to other countries. In 1958 the House Foreign Affairs Committee bluntly asked the State Department, "How much of our aid has been dissipated [in Laos]?" Replied the Department:

"The problem has been one of misdirection and inefficient use of aid rather than dissipation in the true sense. The basic reason for misdirection and inefficient use of aid has been the increasing disparity between the official and black market exchange rates for the kip. . . .

"The major irregularities in the Laos import program have been overinvoicing and diversions. In the former case, importers falsify invoices in order to obtain more foreign exchange than the amount actually necessary to pay for the imports. The difference is easily deposited to their credit in an account outside the country. Diversions occur when goods destined for Laos never get there, or when after arriving in Laos, they are illegally shipped out of the country. . . .

"One of the major contributing factors which accounts for this unsatisfactory situation has been the unrealistic official exchange rate of the kip, which provides a strong incentive for these abuses and affords an opportunity for making illegal profits. This unrealistic rate of the kip is at least partially a reflection of the political instability in that part of the world. As a result there is considerable pressure on the part of those with money to get it out of the country and since this cannot be done officially, it is done largely through the import program."

It took State and ICA some four years to bring the exchange rate in line. Meanwhile, the unrealistic exchange rate, our large cash grants and lax administration of import controls had contributed to the financing of capital flight from a country with a crying need for local capital investment. The House Foreign Operations Subcommittee discovered that ICA had had ample forewarning of the inability of Laos to absorb the flood of dollars we poured into the country. For instance, Howell & Company, a management consulting firm ICA itself had hired, recommended that such difficulties might be avoided if our support of the Laotian Army were paid partly in kind rather than cash.

The Royal Army, however, apparently had other ideas as soon as it learned that Uncle Sam had become its paymaster. Shortly after our aid program began in 1955, the Laos government gave the Army a pay raise amounting to $2.8 million a year. The House subcommittee looked into this, decided the circumstances were at best murky and concluded, "So far as can be determined, the 1955 raise was put into effect by the Royal Laos Government without any consultation with United States aid officials. Presented with an accomplished fact, the United States simply acquiesced."

The Army got itself another royal $1 million-a-year pay raise at the American taxpayers' expense in 1959. This time they asked us first. Somehow the fact that we meant to say "No" made no difference. In August of 1958 our Ambassador cabled Washington that the Laos government had approached him about the pay raise. Washington turned down the request because of the inflationary effect it might have at a time when monetary reform was just getting started. Next try was in December in a cable to the Pacific Commander in Chief, who recommended approval in forwarding the request on to Washington. Again Washington turned thumbs down because the Laotian Army was "already the highest paid group in Laos." This cable went out January 7, 1959.

But on January 5, two days earlier, the Laos government had already announced the pay raise. It did so on the basis of statements from the United States Operations Mission official in Laos who administered the military budget. He had told the Laos government that the raise would be approved provided the overall budget ceiling was not exceeded. This had also been the Pacific Command's recommendation. Later the Mission official explained that up to that time the Pacific Command's approval had been tantamount to Washington's approval. Washington had never before made its decisions known to him directly. Mousetrapped again, Washington went along with the pay raise on the basis of "commitments already made." The House subcommittee noted with some bewilderment:

"Wherever the responsibility for this pay raise lies, and the exact fixing of responsibility is an almost impossible task [as in so many other phases of the foreign aid program], it is costing the United States taxpayers another $1 million a year. It is unfortunate that expenditures of this magnitude can . . . 'just grow,' almost without the conscious intention or attention of any United States official."

Meanwhile, an ICA end-use investigator named Haynes Miller was finding out that it is sometimes very difficult to get official attention when you try to report things running badly. Like investigator Jackis in Cambodia, he discovered that the reward for uncovering waste and inefficiency is sometimes delivered by the back of an official hand.

Miller charged he was harassed and abused for his efforts by administrators up to and including then Ambassador J. Graham Parsons, although some of the irregularities he uncovered eventually led to Federal indictments. Parsons wired the State Department that on August 20, 1957, Miller had been invited by Mission Director Carl Robbins to resign "because of obvious signs of a nervous disorder." Miller's removal from the Mission was based on the obscure catch phrase, "unable to adjust."

The subcommittee, which had heard from Miller and other witnesses, bought neither of these charges. It noted, "If this refers to Miller's ability to adjust to the environment in Laos, it is grossly inaccurate. He was one of the few qualified French linguists at the Mission, probably the most linguistically competent of the American employees. He was also, on the testimony of a number of witnesses, the one who most sought out on a social basis, in a real wish to 'adjust,' Lao and French nationals. . . .

"Ambassador Parsons' opinion of Miller's 'nervous disorder' was rendered without benefit of medical advice. This is contrary to Department of State regulations. Competent medical advice was available to the Ambassador and could have been solicited. This lay medical opinion is particularly noteworthy in that one month later, Miller was subjected to a full medical examination in Washington and certified as 'qualified for general duty.' "

The subcommittee stated its conclusions about Miller's fate even more baldly: "Haynes Miller was 'railroaded' out of Laos because he was close to discovering the truth about Universal, its bribes, its virtual monopoly of United States aid construction projects in Laos, and its woefully inadequate performance."

"Universal" was the Universal Construction Company, Ltd., of Bangkok, formerly headed by Gerald A. Peabody and Willis H. Bird. Along with Edward T. McNamara, the Public Works and Industry officer in Laos at the time of Miller's investigations, they were finally indicted by a Federal grand jury on a charge of conspiring to defraud the United States government. Edward McNamara, it was charged, had accepted bribes of at least $13,000 to help Universal secure contracts and to overlook deficiencies in the company's performance. Among his purported favors was helping Universal get the job of building a ferry ramp on Laos' Mekong River with a bid of $188,755, despite the offer of a rival bidder to do the job for $125,072. McNamara pleaded guilty to the charge in February of 1963. The Justice Department at that time said that Peabody and Bird were believed to be living abroad.

The House subcommittee developed the case on the basis of information that Miller had supplied to the Mission itself —but had little luck getting action on. In fact he had been pulled off the investigation by the Mission controller before he had altogether finished a report dealing with several Universal contracts, including the ferry ramp deal. He was directed to end his probe after, it was charged, Peabody became angry at Miller's effort to examine pertinent Universal records and threatened to have Miller fired.

The subsequently indicted Peabody apparently succeeded in getting Miller's resignation. Ambassador Parsons called Miller in for a twenty-minute conference during which, Miller testified, Parsons "used about fifteen minutes . . . to explain to me how embarrassed he would be if Universal Construction Company was not an honest, straightforward firm, because Washington had asked him earlier in the year if that company was a proper company to receive the contract they were receiving. . . . That left me five minutes to convince an Ambassador who didn't have much faith in me that it was a pretty messy situation."

The subcommittee summarized just how messy the situation was. It found that officials of the United States Operations Mission had "assisted and encouraged the development by the Universal Construction Company of a virtual monopoly of United States-financed construction of projects in Laos."

The former principals of that firm were later indicted for fraud, as indicated above. Investigator Miller had also reported to the Mission that taxpayer-bought road-building equipment entrusted to Universal's care had been abused. He inspected more than a third of the $1.7 million worth of equipment and reported that 94 per cent of the equipment he had seen was either in unsatisfactory condition, or abused, or both—a finding that was later confirmed by a U.S. Bureau of Public Roads official.

The subcommittee found that Universal was paid more than $1.6 million "for performance that was inadequate and did little to enhance the economy of Laos or the prestige of the United States." It was particularly critical of our first two Mission directors in Laos, Carter dePaul and Carl Robbins—the man who "invited" investigator Miller to resign.

The subcommittee's confidence in dePaul was considerably undermined by dePaul's sale of his ten-year-old Cadillac to Universal's obliging Mr. Peabody when dePaul left Laos in 1957. Not even Mr. Robbins liked that deal. According to his testimony, he called it to the attention of the Ambassador, Washington, and even Universal, which he instructed to stop buying cars from Mission personnel. Such purchases, he said, would naturally be suspect. The dePaul deal certainly was.

DePaul's "Cad" was undoubtedly a dog. It would not run. In State Departmentese it was "deadlined" (inoperative). With the cooperation of our Embassy, which obligingly converted the local kips into dollars for dePaul, he got $3,038 for it. This was about three times what he could have got for it on the open market. His father had bought it for him three years earlier in New Jersey—for $800. Robbins and other members of the American colony found it a matter of some embarrassment that the old car just sat around rusting on a Universal lot. It was finally dismembered and dropped down an abandoned well.

There were other odd Mission dealings discovered by the subcommittee.

Item: Norman McKay, an employee of Transportation Consultants, Inc., acting as consultant to the United States Operations Mission, figured in the award of a ferry ramp contract to Universal. Shortly thereafter Universal hired him as a project manager.

Item: Director dePaul once negotiated an upside-down contract with Universal for handling some aid equipment. Work began first, a contract was then signed, bid invitations for the already signed contract were belatedly issued, and finally authorization from Washington was obtained. This was precisely the reverse of procedures set up to protect expenditure of aid money. DePaul also favored Universal by writing two contracts for a single job to evade a rule that a Mission director could not write a contract for more than $25,000 without Washington approval, and wrote up another contract under which Universal was not required to complete any work.

Item: William E. Kirby, area transportation adviser, helped get a ferry barge contract awarded to the Hong Kong Transportation Company and was employed shortly thereafter by the company's affiliate, Pacific Islands Shipbuilding Company. During the contract negotiations Hong Kong Transportation gave Kirby $500, which was "not satisfactorily explained" to the subcommittee.

Item: When Robbins arrived to replace dePaul, he found Mission personnel living in twelve houses so poorly located that during the wet season residents had to wear boots and use boats to get around. These houses had not only cost the United States $30,000 each, but were then costing $300 a month each for maintenance alone. Another contract for twenty-five houses was ramrodded through by a Mission procurement adviser over the objections of an ICA-hired Howell & Company professional consultant. The Howell man found that the deal involved "a group of promoters with no demonstrable ability to complete construction." He turned out to be right. The builder went broke before the houses were finished.

After its long, hard look, the subcommittee concluded, "ICA officials have sought to excuse deficiencies and maladministration in the aid program in Laos, after they have been demonstrated, with the assertion that our aid program, however poorly administered, has saved Laos from going Communist. This assertion is purely speculative, and can be neither proved nor disproved. The subcommittee rejects the reasoning of ICA officials, and, on the evidence, believes that a lesser sum of money more efficiently administered would have been far more effective in achieving economic and political stability in Laos, and in increasing its capacity to reject Communist military aggression or political subversion."

That opinion was delivered in mid-1959. By late 1963 events had done little to change the evaluation. The troika

government that had come into power with the Geneva accord showed few if any signs of pulling the country together.
The International Control Commission's efforts at policing
the truce were feeble at best. Communist, neutralist and pro-
Western factions continued to field their own armies. The
Communist Pathet Lao attacked the neutralists, and battle
raged on the strategic Plaine des Jarres. The West charged
Red China and Communist North Vietnam with continued
help to the guerrilla Pathet Lao. The Red bloc counter-
charged that the United States had violated the Geneva
accord. Whether we had saved Laos from communism was a
question still very much up in the air.

Meanwhile, our pattern of financial aid had done little to
stabilize the Laotian economy. Inflation had slowed business
to a state of somnolence. Japanese radios were selling at four
times what they had sold for a year earlier. Laotian businessmen kept their shops open simply to stave off boredom.

Curiously—and perhaps perversely—this situation was at-
tributed in part to our finally having used our aid dollars
to enforce political decisions. Taking a belatedly harder line,
we had stanched the flood of aid dollars to the former conservative government of Prince Boun Oum to win his government's agreement to the troika policy.

Later we dammed the dollar flow to neutralist Premier
Phouma to prevent misuse of our aid. As a result we won the
unprecedented right to put American customs officials on
the Laotian border to insure that imports were the essential
imports we specified and that speculation in our dollars was
stopped. But the aid cutbacks caused gold and dollar backing of the Laotian kip to drop from 84 to a meager 21 per
cent. The result was inflation.

The authoritative *Wall Street Journal,* daily Bible of the
business world, interpreted these politically motivated checks
to the flow of cash-grant aid as major contributors to the

economic chaos in Laos. The lesson would seem to be that if one force-feeds a fledgling too long, any withdrawal of the bottle will produce economic convulsions. It is clear that our aid policy was not consistent. The writers believe that the hard-line policy should have been followed from the outset. For the inconsistencies have confused not only venal Laos merchants but the honest fellow who bankrolled their peccadilloes—the American taxpayer.

Foreign aid, properly conceived and administered, is not and should not be considered a "rathole." It is, or should be, a dollars-for-security bargain negotiated by a country in its own self-interest. The ultimate failure of diplomacy is death and devastation, the fruits of war. The most compelling reason for a government's expenditure of its wealth as a tool of foreign policy is the prevention of this ultimate failure.

It can be fairly argued that our long-range objectives can be achieved by policies less immediately apparent than use of our money to finance armies willing to fight Communist aggressors within their own countries. It can legitimately be contended that our help in building up a nation's economy might create a climate which, over the long haul, will foster representative government sympathetic to Western, democratic ideals. But there must be some demonstrable results to encourage the American taxpayer to make a continuing investment of his tax dollars to this end.

He is discouraged by evidence of waste of his money by careless or corrupt administrators, whom he pays. He is further discouraged by indications that his economic aid dollars have not appreciably bettered the economy into which they have been so liberally infused, and to that extent have been wasted. And he is most discouraged when, after a decade of spending hundreds of millions of dollars and even losing American lives, the success of his investment is still very much in doubt.

The best possible face that could be put on the Laotian investment was presented by Senate Majority Leader Mansfield and his study group of senators, who reported in February of 1963, "Until the authority of the unified government is generally accepted throughout the country, until the military forces are reduced and unified, the situation is bound to continue to hang in precarious balance. . . . From the point of view of the United States, the situation is improved over that which prevailed when the Geneva Conference convened in 1961.

"At that time it was evident that only military intervention by SEATO, and primarily by United States military forces in considerable strength, in a war of uncertain depth and duration, offered the hope of preventing further deterioration in the position of the Vientiane government. The Geneva Conference interposed a cease-fire at that point, and the accords to which it led helped to forestall a deepening of United States involvement. At least the prospect now exists for a peaceful solution and that alone has already permitted a reduction in both aid costs and numbers of United States personnel in Laos."

But the Presidentially appointed Clay committee a month later voiced a vague belief that even the reduced level of economic assistance was probably too much. "We have not attempted to analyze the substantial costs of our efforts in Laos and Vietnam, since the nature of present United States commitments there precludes useful examination," the Committee reported. "While we recognize that the foreign aid program must be flexible in view of rapid changes in today's world, it was not designed for combat zones; we suggest consideration be given to making provision for such areas other than in our foreign aid program."

Aid expenditures are admittedly risk ventures. A nation does not purchase peace or security as a housewife buys beans—so much per pound. The meaningful expenditure of aid dollars as an instrument of foreign policy is a political art rather than an economic science. But aid expenditures that contribute inadequately to our own recognizable political objectives represent little more than artful waste. That seems to be what the Clay committee was getting at in urging a cutback in Laos.

7 *Languor in Latin America*

Our aid investment in Laos may have been artful waste, but there was nothing even artful about the waste of our aid dollars in the 730-mile-long, Pennsylvania-sized island of Cuba 90 miles off our own Florida coast. It wound up under the heel of a bearded, megalomaniac Communist puppet, Fidel Castro, whose impoverished police state was kept going by $1 million-a-day injections of money from Moscow.

From the end of World War II until we broke off relations with Cuba in early 1961 we invested $52.1 million in aid, $10.6 million of it military. About 90 per cent of the nonmilitary aid was in loans. This, however, was only a fraction of our investment of money, friendship and even American lives over a period extending back into the last century. It was one place where we had little excuse for losing.

Our commitment to Cuba began under the most auspicious circumstances. During the brief Spanish-American War in 1898 we liberated the island from Spain and established an interim military government that helped improve health, education and welfare conditions. In 1901 the Cubans adopted their own constitution and we formally withdrew

106

a year later. The so-called Platt amendment to a 1903 treaty, however, committed us to intervene if Cuban independence was threatened. We did so in 1906 during an internal revolt, but left again in 1909 when a democratic government came to power.

A 1933 revolt led by Army Sgt. Fulgencio Batista left Batista either in power or a power behind the scenes until he was overthrown on the third try by Castro and fled the country in 1959. The Platt amendment had gone out the back door in 1934 after Batista muscled his way to the front. He was a military dictator who ran a corrupt and repressive regime—but we did business with him.

This left us in a somewhat uncertain position when Castro came to power. Did Castro really represent the democratic ideals we should have done more to foster all along, or was he a Communist or a Communist tool? Had our policy been more awake to the legitimate social, economic and political aspirations of Cubans during the Batista years, we might not have had to ask ourselves that question. Castro answered it within a tragically short time. He was, indeed, a Communist and not a very disciplined one at that. Even Moscow found him pretty bizarre.

He nationalized some $1 billion worth of American-owned properties. The United States retaliated by sharply cutting Cuban sugar quotas—a devastating blow to a sugar-dominated economy which we had theretofore bolstered. Communist-bloc countries moved in with aid commitments to help their new Red ally in the Caribbean. The abortive United States-backed Bay of Pigs invasion by Cuban exiles shortly after President Kennedy took office served only to entrench Castro and arm him with a new excuse for echoing the old charge of "Yankee imperialism." We paid $54 million in ransom for return of the 1,113 Cuban freedom fighters Castro seized in that fiasco.

Encouraged by evidence of United States indecision and/ or timidity, the Soviet Union began moving her own "technicians," war matériel, military planes and offensive ballistic missiles into Cuba, insisting that the conventional equipment was only for Cuban defense and denying that missiles were even present. Our reconnaissance photography proved them liars. There followed the tensest week of the Cold War.

On October 22, 1962, President Kennedy called Russia's hand. He demanded removal of the offensive missiles and dismantling of the missile sites. He warned bluntly that any nuclear missile attack from Cuba on the Americas would bring nuclear retaliation on Russia itself, and announced a naval blockade of arms shipments into Cuba that began two days later. On October 28 Soviet Premier Khrushchev announced that he had ordered the sites dismantled and the missiles returned to Russia. Soviet jet bombers were also sent back.

The world breathed a deep sigh. Nuclear devastation had been rejected as an extreme merited by the Cuban situation. But the Cold War was in no sense thawed. By the very rejection of the ultimate nuclear horror, positions had become further frozen in the hemisphere. Under attack from its fractious Red Chinese ally for appeasing the West, Russia could not back off from its commitment to Cuba. And we obviously could not accommodate ourselves to the Communist presence within the Western Hemisphere. We had, in fact, already sacrificed considerable prestige by ignoring the spirit of the Monroe Doctrine, which banned foreign domination of a hemisphere neighbor.

The importance of the Cuban situation to our foreign aid thesis, however, lies less in the developing details of the story than in its impact on our foreign aid policy in Latin America. It underscored our earlier shocked discovery that the so-called "revolution of rising expectations" in Latin America had been significantly infiltrated by the Communists. This was brought home hard to most Americans for the first time, perhaps, in 1958 when Vice-President Richard M. Nixon was stoned by a Communist mob during a visit to Caracas, Venezuela.

What had gone wrong in the picturesque Southern continent, the relaxed land where chores could be done *mañana*, the scene of happy fiestas recorded on the home movie films of visiting North Americans? Actually, there was nothing sudden about it. South American leaders had been trying for years to tell us that our tourist impressions were superficial fiction.

In the early fifties the United Nations Economic Commission for Latin America had proposed an overall approach to social and economic needs in the hemisphere. The Latin countries themselves in 1954 had asked the United States to establish an Inter-American Development Bank, the regional equivalent of the World Bank. We said no. In 1958 Brazil's respected President Juscelino Kubitschek proposed an "Operation Panamerica" program of social and economic development which would represent "a new orientation of continental political affairs." The Nixon stoning jolted us into action.

The Inter-American Development Bank came into being in 1960. In the 1960 Act of Bogotá, the United States and sister American states entered on an inter-American aid program. Said then Under Secretary of State Douglas Dillon, "The government of the United States is prepared to devote over the years ahead large additional resources to the inauguration and carrying forward of a broad new social development program for Latin America, dedicated to supporting the self-help efforts of the governments and peoples of Latin America." Congress authorized $500 million for the program.

With President Kennedy came the Alliance for Progress,

an outgrowth of these preceding developments. The actual Alliance was first proposed March 13, 1961, in an address to Latin American Ambassadors in the White House. The Alliance for Progress, the President proposed, would launch "a vast new ten-year plan for the Americas, a plan to transform the 1960s into a historic decade of democratic progress." On August 17, 1961, nineteen Latin American republics and the United States signed the Charter of Punta del Este (Uruguay) and the Alliance for Progress was born.

By its second birthday, the United States had committed $2.18 billion and actually disbursed $1.5 billion to the Alliance. Nearly 400 separate projects were under way. They ranged from housing projects to economic planning and educational, medical and social welfare aid, all carried out in cooperation with local governments and private groups which matched the United States aid in varying degrees.

Two weeks after the Alliance's second birthday, the United States coordinator of the program, Teodoro Moscoso, gave this report to the Commonwealth Club of California:

. . . Planning for development has got under way in every member country of the Alliance. Seven countries have submitted blueprints for marshaling their internal resources and effectively utilizing external assistance. In eleven Latin American countries, tax reforms are under way. In many cases, income and property taxes are being applied for the first time in a country's history. . . .

Landholding problems have received more attention than at any time since the Wars of Independence of Latin America. Prior to the signing of the Alliance charter, only Mexico, Bolivia and Venezuela had basic agrarian reform legislation. Since its signing, five more countries have adopted laws and started on land redistribution schemes. Five other countries are now studying the most effective and appropriate method to raise both productivity and living standards on the land. . . .

Perhaps the most fundamental series of reforms . . . has been in education. The Latin American countries have substantially increased their budget allocations to education and have taken other significant stages to develop their most valuable resource— people. All of the hemisphere's resources could be poured into primary education without coming to grips with its need for qualified engineers, economists, professional men and technicians needed to staff government and industry, to draft and execute national plans and to develop a productive agriculture. Latin America has an estimated fifty thousand engineers and technicians in a population larger than our own, while we have over a million and feel we suffer a shortage. . . .

We are seeking a balance between primary and higher education. In the first two years of the Alliance, more than eight thousand new classrooms have been built—and teachers trained to use them. Nearly four million textbooks have been distributed—often the first books of their kind ever received by the children. We are supporting technical training programs for workers in a score of countries, ranging from apprenticeship in El Salvador and industrial training in Chile to vocational education in Brazil and Ecuador.

Other gains cited by Moscoso included 140,000 new homes, 1,500 water systems and wells, 900 hospitals and health centers built, 160,000 farm credit loans issued. But both Moscoso and President Kennedy recognized that these were comparatively tiny drops in an enormous bucket of need. Much more would be needed over a period longer than a decade to better significantly the impoverished fortunes of some 210,000,000 Latin Americans. Commented the President after two years of the Alliance, "We have a long, long way to go, and in fact in some ways the road seems longer than it was when the journey started." Conceded Moscoso, "The job will by no means be finished by 1970. The political, economic and social transformation of a continent is not accomplished overnight. What we must seek to provide rapidly is evidence of progress which can sustain the hopes of the people and thus provide the opportunity to complete the long-term task."

There was some question, however, whether the evidence or rate of progress was dramatic enough to sustain such hopes. Editorial Research Reports, a Washington news service, opened its analysis of the Alliance's second birthday with the observation that "doubt, disappointment and disdain" colored the observance. The *New York Times* Latin American correspondent, Juan de Onis, wrote from Lima that a survey "revealed widespread public disenchantment or listlessness toward the Alliance for Progress as a concept or as an operative program. This was further reflected in comments by political leaders that were mainly critical of the results obtained."

There were several reasons for this attitude, the most ironic of which was that the Alliance for Progress was more soundly conceived than most of our aid programs had been. This was not another Laotian venture, in which we would siphon aid dollars wholesale through weak or corrupt governments into economies too simple to absorb what trickled down. It was a cooperative ten-year, $20 billion venture in social and economic reform, from which we hoped political stability would emerge. It was a self-help program. We would guarantee at least $10 billion in aid, but it would be predicated on efforts within the countries themselves to initiate the reforms that would make the use of the aid meaningful.

Many Latins failed to understand that this was not simply another Uncle Sam giveaway. This failure was reflected in Moscoso's report that after two years only seven of the nineteen countries had yet submitted blueprints for effective use of the aid. Others may have been bewildered by the variety of goals the Alliance had set—housing programs, agrarian reform, fair wages and working conditions, eradication of illiteracy, improved health and sanitation, tax reform, price stabilization, integration of the Latin American economy. This was, indeed, a tall order for a continent which for generations had struggled along under generally weak or dictatorial governments. But the drama and optimism with which the program was launched raised Latin American hopes beyond its ability to realize them.

By December 1963, nobody really had any new ideas about what should be done about Latin America, but President Johnson did give the policy a new look. He named Thomas C. Mann Assistant Secretary of State for Latin American Affairs, and a few days later gave Mann another title, that of Special Assistant to the President. Apparently, the President wanted Foggy Bottom to read him loud and clear when he noted that he was determined to make sure the United States spoke "with one voice" on all matters affecting Latin America. Mann's second title obviously was a warning to the cutthroats in the State Department that he was under the special protection of the White House and that any sabotage of his efforts would be viewed sternly by the Big Boss himself. Mann, who was Ambassador to Mexico at the time of his appointment, was regarded as a diplomat who "knows how to get along with Latins." He had grown up in Texas along the Mexican border, and for many years he had been prominent in movements aimed at the economic and social progress of Latin America. But since Mann was human, his task of trying to make sense out of the chaotic Alliance for Progress was perhaps the toughest tackled by any American diplomat.

Three organizations share responsibility for conduct of the program. One is the Organization of American States, chartered in 1948. It was at a conference of OAS's economic and social council that the Alliance for Progress was created. A panel of nine OAS international experts evaluates the development plans submitted by Latin American governments to qualify for Alliance aid. The second organization is the Inter-American Development Bank, the lending agency through which aid is funneled. The third is the United Nations Economic Commission, which provides and trains development specialists, gives research and planning aid, and helps stimulate regional economic integration.

This studied approach toward helping our South American neighbors far exceeded anything we had attempted earlier. Historically, our foreign policy had taken Latin America into account. The Monroe Doctrine, the Pan American Regional Organization, President Roosevelt's Good Neighbor policy, President Truman's Point Four plan, our leading role in the OAS—all attested to our interest. But the Alliance for Progress surpassed all of our previous efforts both in the extent of financial commitment and in breadth of objective.

The challenge of its socio-economic goals was enormous. And nowhere was the challenge more apparent than in Haiti, Cuba's Caribbean neighbor, where 90 per cent of the adults were illiterate, the average per capita income was about $70 per year, and where government by terror was presided over by a voodoo-practicing doctor-dictator named François Duvalier. Despite our injection of some $53 million in aid over an eight-year period, the per capita income was the lowest in the hemisphere. Between 1960 and 1962 we had shipped some $1.1 million of military equipment into Haiti. Finally, Alliance or no, we could not stand Duvalier's sinister police state and stanched the flow of wasted aid in 1962—or so it was announced.

But in foreign aid there always seem to be some inconsistent loose ends lying about. It was not until the summer of 1963, nearly six months after "termination" of aid, that one of these loose ends was discovered by Senator Karl Mundt, the toy bulldog Republican from South Dakota. In quizzing Aid Director David Bell, Mundt brought out that there had been three exceptions to the cutoff. Mundt found no quarrel with two of these: a loan of $250,000 to an American company for expansion of a sisal plantation and factory, which had been signed in 1961, and support for a malaria eradication program which was a problem for the region rather than for one country.

Mundt literally saw red when he learned that the third exception was a loan for construction of an airport capable of receiving jet planes. "I am concerned about this airport," muttered Mundt. "It can very well become an airport in which Castro or Russia can land planes, probably as easily or perhaps more easily than a freedom-loving country like ours. Such assistance tends to discredit our entire AID program."

A week later, the State Department had an announcement for the press. It read, simply, "The United States informed the government of Haiti today that the Agency for International Development has suspended all activities to implement the loan agreement for construction of a new jet airport for Port au Prince, Haiti."

In the grand plan for helping Latin America, Haiti was an especially horrible example of an impossible situation. But in seven other Latin American nations the adult illiteracy rate was 50 per cent or more. In Bolivia, Peru, Costa Rica, El Salvador, Honduras, Paraguay and Ecuador, the annual per capita income was under $200. In Bolivia, Brazil, Venezuela and Ecuador, governments were at best unstable. One-crop economies left many of our Latin American neighbors vulnerable to the slightest shifts in world trade and, therefore, vulnerable to ensuing political unrest.

Coffee, for instance, provided most of the export earnings of Guatemala, El Salvador and Colombia. Copper provided 65.7 per cent of Chile's export earnings; 92 per cent of Venezuela's earnings were from oil; 68.5 per cent of Bolivia's earnings came from tin; 62.9 per cent of Uruguay's earnings came from wool. Bananas accounted for 54.5 per cent of Nicaragua's export earnings.

Such severe economic handicaps, linked with political instability and/or almost feudal social patterns in some countries, offered stony soil in which to sow the seeds of aid-financed reform. Some critics of the Alliance for Progress said flatly that it would not work. One such was John Paton Davies, Jr., a Lima businessman and former United States foreign service officer who had been stationed in Latin America. In the *New York Times Magazine* of August 25, 1963, he wrote:

The Kennedy Administration's resolve to push reform is unexceptionable in moral intent. But it is politically naïve and inoperable. The determination to make over the Latin-American social structure has aroused suspicion, when not hostility, without attracting in the area a strong alignment of supporters. The two most powerful elements—the rich and the military—suspect that the *Alianza* is a Yankee maneuver to diminish their influence. In this they are not far wrong.

As for an upsurge of popular support, Dr. Lleras Camargo, former President of Colombia and an ardent supporter of the *Alianza*, summed it up in June: "The truth is that one cannot see anywhere in Latin America the spirit of enthusiasm that should precede and go along with such a formidable adventure."

The Administration, apparently, had not thought through the implications of its policy. If one advocates a crash program to upset an established social order, resistance should be anticipated. And if the undertaking is serious, then one should be willing and prepared to follow through to overcome the resistance when encountered. But this, on belated second thought, our Government seems unwilling to do. And quite rightly so. For to try to force through the reforms would reduce our relations with the rest of the hemisphere to a shambles, without attaining the ends sought.

The fact was that as of the fall of 1963 six elected Latin American governments had been toppled in a period of eighteen months, and in each case the military either initiated the revolt or shaped its outcome. The military, some of them trained in the United States, were behind the ouster of duly elected civilian governments in Argentina, Peru, Guatemala, Ecuador, the Dominican Republic and Honduras. The old South-of-the-Border habit of effecting change through junta-backed revolt seemed to bode ill for the Alliance's effort to counter Cuba's sad example with proof that constitutional government could bring social reform. The administration adopted a policy of aid withdrawal from junta-controlled countries. But it also sought to put the best possible face on the military take-overs, professing to find in them signs of greater concern than of old for the public weal.

There was a possibility the administration was not merely rationalizing about an unattractive situation in thus finding some good in the military. Even as the juntas were having their way with those unhappy countries, a little-known United States-financed project in the Panama Canal Zone was toiling at the chore of reforming the military.

The project was the United States Army's School of the Americas, designed primarily to train selected officers and men from Latin American armies in the rough-and-ready art of protecting their countries from Communist subversion. The students were tutored in jungle warfare, riot work and the niceties of infiltrating and disrupting secret terrorist bands. But, as Rowland Evans and Robert Novak noted in the New York *Herald Tribune,* "the school's value may go beyond this. It could help transform the Latin American army, long allied with church and oligarchy in a reactionary trinity, into a progressive institution."

This dream is based on the "extras" in the school's curriculum—courses in "civic action" at which the students learned how to build roads, assist youth groups and generally participate in civilian community life. As a result, the peasants in the interior of several Latin American republics enjoyed the unprecedented experience of having detachments of military roar into their villages to build basketball courts, community centers, schools and even pits for cockfights. It was perhaps too soon to expect the military to develop a social conscience, but in the Canal Zone a start had been made in trying to make it live up to Davies' appraisal of it.

Davies' argument, of course, was based on a belief that the military in Latin America are a patriotic and stabilizing influence and that the rich have, by and large, met their socioeconomic obligations. The authors have cited his view to underline the difficulties the Alliance faces. They do not subscribe to his whole argument. It seems clear that if American aid dollars are to be used to fight Communism, they must buy some change in those social patterns that Communism would find most ready targets. To call for meaningful reform without calling for some change in social patterns would seem to be self-contradictory.

One might buy that portion of Mr. Davies' argument that insisted that the most constructive way we could help would be by aiding economic development, improving management and labor techniques, removing as best we can impediments to foreign trade, and realizing that "there are humbling limitations on what we can do to help in so turbulent and alien a situation." Evidence by late 1963 indicated that Moscoso and the Alliance people recognized these limitations, and with the help of United States labor, farm and management groups, were working toward most of these objectives.

The Presidential Clay committee also took a hard look at

the Alliance program after a year and a half of operation and concluded: "Latin American understanding of and willingness to fulfill the undertakings of leadership, self-help and self-discipline agreed to in the Punta del Este charter . . . with notable exceptions have yet to be proved." The committee warned that no amount of outside aid would speed progress "if Latin American leaders do not stimulate the will for development, mobilize internal savings, encourage the massive flow of private investment, and promote other economic, social and administrative changes."

The committee found some evidence that the United States was doing too much of the job already. It recommended against United States financing of local costs of the programs within the recipient country, either directly or through the Inter-American Development Bank except on an interim basis. Even on an interim basis, the committee said, the aid should not be so lavish that the recipient government would be deterred from raising its own funds for the job. Said the committee:

"The United States should continue to make unmistakably clear that the Alliance for Progress is a long-term venture of extraordinary complexity and scope, demanding a decade or more of sustained effort by all involved to attain truly significant results. Accordingly, the United States will not accept empty praise or unjustified criticism of the Alliance as substitutes for Latin American performance. Also, the American public should cease to judge the Alliance on whether it has accomplished in two years what must take much longer. Indeed, care must be taken even now to assure that United States assistance does not exceed amounts that can be usefully absorbed without encouraging even less effort and discipline on the part of governments to the south. It should be recognized that demand for rapid results could lead to expenditures which would ultimately defeat their purpose. . . ."

The United States should be "increasingly more specific on the self-help and reforms it seeks and do so on a country-by-country basis. . . . Assistance should be concentrated heavily on those countries which undertake to meet the principles established in the charter of Punta del Este," the committee recommended.

What the Clay committee recommended, in short, was a hard-nosed policy which would reward those nations which effected reforms, or at least set up the local machinery to effect them, and put at the bottom of our aid list those nations which were less responsive. The authors concur with this finding. Without such a firm policy the Alliance program will produce what less well-defined programs have spawned elsewhere—pure waste. Firmness is particularly important in Latin American countries where vested interests in effect run the government and have a personal stake in maintaining the status quo. Political scientist Hans Morgenthau discusses the dangers inherent in foreign aid commitments of this type:

The ownership and control of arable land, in particular, is in many of the underdeveloped societies the foundation of political power. Land reform and industrialization are in consequence an attack upon the political status quo. In the measure that they succeed, they are bound to affect drastically the distribution of economic and political power alike. Yet the beneficiaries of both the economic and political status quo are the typical recipients of foreign aid given for the purpose of changing the status quo. To ask them to use foreign aid for this purpose is to require a readiness for self-sacrifice and a sense of social responsibility which few ruling groups have shown throughout history. Foreign aid proffered under such circumstances . . . is more likely to accentuate unsolved social and political problems than to bring them closer to solution.

Morgenthau sees yet other possible dangers in economic aid to underdeveloped countries. Suppose the donor nation succeeds in changing the status quo. Can it also succeed in finding or encouraging the right kind of successors to the powers that be? And if land reform and industrialization are brought about, might they not whet the native appetite for even more far-reaching reforms? Might not Communism then exploit this eager appetite with its false promises of instant progress? These, he warns, are questions that had best be taken into account before economic development aid is offered as a certain technique for thwarting communism.

This scholarly warning serves to underscore again the difference between our Alliance for Progress effort and the self-help Marshall Plan, after which it was in part patterned. With an envious glance at Europe's prosperous Common Market, the charter of Punta del Este called for "economic integration" in Latin America. Two groups are emerging. One is the Central American common market composed of Costa Rica, El Salvador, Guatemala, Honduras and Nicaragua. The other is the so-called Latin American Free Trade Association, including Argentina, Brazil, Chile, Colombia, Ecuador, Mexico, Paraguay, Peru and Uruguay. Neither group, of course, has moved forward with anything like the dispatch of the European Economic Community, which was the natural fruit of a high degree of political stability, economic organization and social cohesion within the member countries. None of these advantages is present in significant degree throughout Latin America.

So it was that the *New York Times* observed the Alliance's second birthday with this observation: "The wonder is not that the Alliance for Progress has accomplished so little in two years, but that it has done so much under such great difficulties. It needs and deserves continued support and encouragement. For all its weaknesses, no one has come up with a better idea. The choice for Latin America remains what it has been: violent revolution of the Castro type or evolution under the Alliance for Progress."

Beyond the sheer physical enormity of the task, there were at least two other reasons for the slow advance of the program. One was the lack of private investment capital, which the program counted on to spur economic development. Neither local, United States or other foreign capital was invested at the hoped-for rate, and, in fact, investment declined. Blame for this rested with the Latin tendency to overtax foreign investors, in some cases to expropriate foreign property, and to favor the public sector of the economy.

A second reason was more heartening to the United States taxpayer. It was simply that a good many pleas for loans and grants were rejected outright or postponed because they were ill-conceived or ill-planned. One could only hope that the program's administrators would continue in this happy tradition, putting aside whatever temptations might present themselves to approve hastily dreamed-up "impact" projects meant to demonstrate that the Alliance works instant miracles.

8 *India-Pakistan:*
A Costly Paradox

Shortly before he died, John F. Kennedy said, "We must recognize that we cannot remake the world simply by our own command. We must recognize that every nation determines its policy in terms of its own interest. . . . The purpose of foreign policy is not to provide an outlet for our own sentiments of hope or indignation. It is to shape real events in a real world. . . . To adopt a black-and-white, all-or-nothing policy subordinates our interests to our irritations."

This recognition comes hard to most Americans. It has been made no easier by watching some $5 billion of our aid over a period of little more than a decade flow hopefully into a neutral country with the irritating habit of being frequently "neutral" in favor of our foes. This is India, the teeming, impoverished underbelly of the Asian continent where the spiraling birthrate has threatened to overwhelm even the most ambitious plans for economic development.

A place of vast paradox, India was the bailiwick of Prime Minister Jawaharlal Nehru, who could at once be outraged by arrant Red Chinese violations of India's northern frontier and champion Red China's admission to the supposedly peaceful fraternity of the United Nations. As a former British colony, India could work itself up into a frenzy about the evils of colonialism while pukka Indians, speaking in Oxford tones, strove mightily to sustain the parliamentary traditions of the British political system. A "nonviolent" oasis in a violent world, India could and did forcefully seize outright the Portuguese colonies of Goa, Damão and Diu and battle with neighboring Pakistan for possession of Kashmir.

Moreover, Nehru's own words have made him suspect among Americans as a wistful observer of the Communist world. "I have in mind a definitely, absolutely socialist picture of society," he has said. And, "I had long been drawn to socialism and communism, and Russia appealed to me. . . . The Communist philosophy of life gave me comfort and hope . . ." And, in his autobiography, "I incline more and more towards Communist philosophy."

Nehru supported the motion in the United Nations naming North Korea the aggressor in the 1950 "incident" which first resulted in a "police action" by the UN and then developed into a full-scale hot war. But his contribution to Allied forces in Korea was barely a token—one ambulance unit. The Indian representative on the Neutral Nations Commission charged with handling the prisoner-of-war problem cast the decisive vote which permitted the Reds to write the brainwashing rules to coerce prisoners into returning to the Communist camp. Nehru, of course, meanwhile was arguing that there would have been no Korean War if the West had not refused to seat Red China in the UN.

Yet the United States, in behalf of the self-interest which hopefully works to keep India from being too "neutral" in favor of Communism, has continued to heap largesse on this politically neurotic mystic. Often, Nehru has not even been required to ask for help, as during his Gettysburg meeting with President Eisenhower in December, 1956. Eisenhower raised the subject of India's economic future and told Nehru that India's second "five-year plan" was a good one and "I want to boost it." It seems the State Department had suggested that Nehru might be too timid to broach the matter—and apparently we just had to give him some money.

By 1963 India had jumped to first place among recipients of American economic aid. We were pouring in loans and grants at a rate of $725 million a year, or more than $1.50 for each of India's 450,000,000 people. Since AID was formed in 1961 as a "holding company" to coordinate our various assistance programs, India had received more than $1 billion in economic help, most of it in long-term loans, and another $60 million in military aid to fend off Red Chinese border aggressions.

Since 1957 India had bought nearly 20 million tons of our surplus food and 1.4 billion bales of our surplus fiber. These were mostly wheat and cotton. But under terms of our Public Law 480, which governs distribution of our surpluses abroad, 80 per cent of the sales proceeds reverted to India in grants and loans, which came to the equivalent of about $1 billion. With these funds India financed health, education, power and agricultural programs. Since 1951 we had spent $100 million on technical aid to India, sending American experts there and bringing Indian students to the United States. We had contributed another $90 million to the effort to wipe out malaria in India. And since 1958 the Export-Import Bank had also loaned India $307 million to pay for American imports to meet domestic needs.

Our aid commitments had been vastly more generous—both in amount and in the terms on which it was offered—than the $1 billion Soviet-bloc contributions, but the Soviets were also obviously wooing India and even came through with military aid for defense against the incursions of Russia's erstwhile Chinese comrades. This indicated that India's neutral, nonalignment policy was indeed serving India's "own interest," as President Kennedy suggested that foreign policy should. But was our policy of lavishing aid on India serving our interests?

Our hard-core interest in granting aid anywhere is to thwart the imperialist ambitions of world Communism. Economic aid is meant to further the donee's plans for curing those socio-economic ills upon which Communism preys from within. Military aid is meant to ward off aggression from without. Although almost all of our aid to India had been economic, a substantial amount of our more than $3 billion in aid to her neighbor, Pakistan, was military. In each case, it was meant to serve our interests in containing Communism, of either the Soviet or the Chinese variety.

But our aid was caught in the crosscurrents of India-Pakistan enmity, and to the extent that it failed to achieve its full purpose, some of it may prove to have been misspent. In brief, this was the situation: Communist China was our enemy. Nonaligned India and our ally, Pakistan, were enemies. Pakistan disliked and distrusted India more than she did Communist China and was actually working toward a *rapprochement* with the Chinese—the exact opposite of what we had conceived to be our interest in granting aid to Pakistan.

India-Pakistan enmity was born and rose like an evil phoenix from the ashes of the British Empire. Before Britain pulled out of the subcontinent in 1947, she divided it up by creating the new and predominantly Moslem state of Pakistan. This new state, in turn, was monstrously split. East Pakistan, rich in natural resources, lies on one side of predominantly Hindu India. West Pakistan, the economic and political center, lies 1,000 miles away on India's other flank. Nearly a million died in the Moslem-Hindu slaughter that attended the scramble of each to find a home within the newly defined boundaries.

Immediately the state of Kashmir, situated between West Pakistan and India, became a sore in which India-Pakistan relations have festered ever since. Each claimed it. Pakistan first moved in her troops. India then seized Kashmir's fertile heartland, the Vale. India's claim was based on the fact that the Hindu Maharaja had acceded to India in 1947 after fighting between the two countries broke out. But southern Kashmir was heavily Moslem and would almost certainly have voted to join Pakistan if it had been put to a vote. The United Nations fixed a cease-fire line as early as 1949, but by late 1963 no accommodation had been reached.

Our arms commitment to Pakistan resulted from the search early in the Eisenhower administration for alliances through which Communism could be contained. The results of this quest by Secretary of State John Foster Dulles included the Baghdad Pact, or Central Treaty Organization (CENTO) and the Southeast Asia Treaty Organization (SEATO). Pakistan became our ally and partner in both and as a result received such modern equipment as supersonic jet fighters, tactical missiles and late-model tanks. Pakistan, however, was more mindful of their value in the bitter feud with India than for use against the Red Chinese, with whom she had had no special quarrel.

When in the winter of 1962 Red China launched its attack on nonaligned India's northern frontier, the reactions of "allied" Pakistan and the United States were dramatically dissimilar. Pakistan began to find the Red Dragon a rather friendly beast. The United States was further convinced that it was just beastly, and, with other Western allies, launched a program of military aid to India. Although it was only a fraction (some $60 million) of the military hardware we had given Pakistan, it was enough to make Pakistan both apprehensive and resentful. Pakistan, with only about one-fifth of India's population, felt that military aid would further augment India's odds in any India-Pakistan clash. Assurances that our aid to India was meant only for defense against the Chinese did little to mollify popular Pakistan resentment.

Peking types became conspicuous in Pakistan. Less than two months after our military aid to India was under way, a long-standing Sino-Pakistan border issue was amicably settled to Pakistan's advantage. There followed a Chinese-Pakistan trade agreement and a pact for the exchange of commercial airline services. Pakistan President Ayub Khan, in short, was finding that the new struggle between the Western and Communist blocs had strengthened his own bargaining position. United States aid was supplying some 40 per cent of the country's day-to-day budget and 80 per cent of its "development" budget. The Red Chinese, eager to exploit India-Pakistan enmity, came now with their own goodies.

Washington reacted with understandable pique to the Pakistan-Chinese air pact. It "postponed" a four-point $3 million loan for airport improvements at Dacca, East Pakistan, where the Pakistan government had granted landing rights to Chinese Communist aircraft. Promptly, President Ayub adopted the wonted attitude of the poor relative who resents the necessity of accepting largesse from a rich uncle. Pakistan, he declared, had always accepted foreign aid on the understanding that it was offered without strings, but if it was found that American aid required a *quid pro quo,* then his government would be forced to reconsider its policy toward accepting such help. He hinted that Pakistan might have to enter into a military treaty with Red China unless Uncle Sam behaved himself.

Americans encouraged by this show of firmness by their government found their satisfaction short-lived, however.

Less than a month later, on September 27, 1963, Washington announced that the United States and Pakistan had signed a $70 million loan agreement for iron, steel and other American products. And despite the loan, Ayub made it clear that his government would continue its policy of seeking improved relations with the Communist bloc. On the same day the American loan was sealed, Pakistan signed barter agreements under which it would receive 100,000 tons of cement from the Soviet Union and 30,000 tons of cement from Poland in exchange for jute of equal value.

This left us in the anomolous position of having put most of our military aid in the hands of an ally least likely to use it against our real enemy, Red China. Our aid emphasis began shifting to our non-ally, India. Yet jealously nonaligned India, even in its hour of peril, had some qualms about accepting our arms. Economic assistance could be justified on the willing Indian assumption that it was the duty of wealthy democracies to help their impoverished but politically sympathetic kin with vast outlays of gifts and credit. But with colonialism held in recent and bitter memory, India sought to shun even the appearance of any seduction by the West with arms aid and promptly set out to negotiate arms deals with the Soviet bloc as well.

It will remain for history to say what wisdom or folly motivated United States policy in the Asian subcontinent. Scholars sympathetic to India's plight, however, point out that United States impatience with India's nonalignment policy ignores our own history. We too, at the birth of our nation, eschewed "foreign entanglements" and enjoyed the protection of the Atlantic and Pacific Oceans in efforts to hew to that resolve. It was, in fact, only after World War II that we really broke out of our isolationist shell onto the center of the world political stage.

Thus, Indian apologists argue, it is inconsistent for us to

be put out with a nation, barely recovered from the pangs of its own birth, for its refusal to ally itself with us as an adult partner in our global enterprises. History may show that the United States benefited as much or more from India's non-alignment than from the aid dollars we spent there. India's nonalignment had brought about a coup that our own most brilliant strategists had not been able to bring off. This was the pitting of Communism against itself—Soviet-bloc sympathy for quelling Red Chinese aggression. The full extent and nature of Soviet military aid—and the political price tag that would attach to it—were unclear by late 1963. But it did seem clear that any substantial Soviet military commitment would be aimed as much at freezing Western influence out of India as blocking Chinese expansion into it.

Our economic aid to India posed other and quite different questions, which go to the heart of foreign aid theory. The first question is whether vast economic investment will produce a politically palatable return. Some students argue that in tragically underdeveloped countries like India the most generous aid can at best offer only a taste of a better life. The native appetite, once whetted, then feeds on dissatisfaction with the pace of progress. And Communism is offered an opportunity to exploit this dissatisfaction for its own subversive ends.

The awesome statistics of Indian poverty hardly need retelling. It had an annual average wage of some $70. Only 35 per cent of its population was literate. The poverty and ignorance were compounded by the birthrate. Sixteen years after India became independent it had an additional 100,-000,000 mouths to feed. Its society, divided into some 3,000 subcastes, made America's racial problem seem a charade of simplicity.

Our substantial economic aid effort indicated, therefore, that we believed that even these odds were beatable. Or, at least, that the investment was producing some immediate return. The Clay committee found, for instance, that India had proved "that it is determined to maintain its independence from Communist domination. Together with our ally, Pakistan, it is the only area of South Asia able to offset the Red Chinese colossus.

"Unless their freedom and economic growth continue, there can never be a balance of power in Asia and our own involvement in this area could be indefinite and infinitely more costly. Thus, we believe that in the interest of our own and free world security, economic and military assistance to India, as well as to Pakistan, must continue under present circumstances. However, it would be difficult to justify continued economic assistance at present rates unless other free world countries continue and extend their support on terms comparable to our own."

Assuming, then, that large aid investment in areas of such overwhelming need is justified, there arises the further question about the conditions we put upon our offers. Obviously the offers should be conditioned on use of the money for purposes that will advance our interests—to fight Communism or to improve the socio-economic climate within the donee country so that Communism cannot subvert it. But must the aid be funneled through the classic American machinery of private investment? The Clay committee had something to say about this, too:

"AID has shown increasing awareness of the vital role played by local and foreign private investment in the development process, but fuller cognizance is required in conceiving, conditioning and implementing its programs in various countries. . . . Our conviction is based not on doctrine but on the practical realization that it is the private sector, operating with the cooperation of a vital and democratic labor movement and enlightened management on the basis of essential government services and sensible policies, which will make the greatest contribution to rapid economic growth and overall development."

As a general principle for use of our aid in countries where experienced entrepreneurs, a "vital and democratic labor movement, and enlightened management" abound, the Clay committee's recommendation is probably faultless. But as a rigid standard for helping underdeveloped areas where these factors are absent or inadequate, it is overly doctrinaire. This was the crux of the controversy over India's proposed Bokaro steel mill some 150 miles northwest of Calcutta.

India wanted the United States to contribute some $900 million over a period of fourteen years toward the cost of the mill, which would eventually have an annual capacity of some 4 million tons of flat steel. The mill would eventually pay for itself in savings that would accrue from India's not having to import steel. The United States aid would not represent an additional commitment, but a diversion of our commitment from other Indian projects to the mill. Although the mill was to be publicly owned, private steel producers urged its construction, conceding that it was beyond the capacity of the private sector of India's steel industry to build it. Other private business interests in India also favored the project.

Not so the United States House of Representatives. In the fiscal 1964 foreign aid authorization bill, the House specifically killed off United States participation. The basic complaint, beyond the size of the commitment, was that it was "socialistic." The Clay committee's recommendation about fostering the private sector of the economies of donee nations figured prominently in the debate. Although India urgently wanted United States aid for the mill and President Kennedy had endorsed the project, India formally withdrew its request following the House action to preclude further ruffling of India-United States relations.

Once having made a judgment that our interest requires aid to underdeveloped nations, it seems self-defeating to insist that development of a badly needed basic industry must follow the same path in New Delhi that it does in Dover, Delaware. We have recognized this even within our own borders. There is, for instance, a "mix" in our approach to power production. Private power companies supply most of the electricity that lights American homes and runs American factories. But Congress in the early 1930s chose to give to a government agency, the Tennessee Valley Authority, the task of developing an "underdeveloped" section of the United States. Except for a last-century lunatic fringe, Congress recognizes this bold experiment as one of its proudest creations. Prosperity in the Tennessee Valley has resulted in increased tax yields to the Treasury. And TVA itself is making repayments to the Treasury from its electric power proceeds on the taxpayer investment in its operations. TVA has proved, in fact, to be not only a "must" on the list of things visiting foreigners wish to see but a sound investment for the country.

Among those who had favored United States participation in the Bokaro project was our former Ambassador to India, John Kenneth Galbraith. Writing in the Washington *Post* of August 18, 1963, he offered this cogent analysis of the problem of being too doctrinaire:

The Communists offer public ownership, or socialism, and excoriate private ownership. If we excoriate public ownership, and insist in an equally dogmatic way on private capitalism, we leave those who believe deeply in democratic socialism no choice but to align themselves with the Communists. This is a mistake we have made in the past and which we have rectified in India with real gains for our position.

We know from experience in Scandinavia, Great Britain, Canada, New Zealand, and even our own past that a pragmatic combination of public and private ownership is quite compatible with personal liberty. If we offer a broad choice in economic organization as against the narrow Communist choice we cannot lose. If we offer a narrow alternative of a specific form of private capitalism to the narrow Communist choice we could lose.

This is not an academic issue. The Communists have been having a difficult time in India. The Chinese attack cost them heavily. They have been quick to seize upon gleams of daylight. The Clay Committee report, with its implied criticism of support to public enterprises, was greeted with unalloyed enthusiasm by the Indian left-wing press last spring. They took it as proof that the democratic socialists had no future on our side. As I cabled at the time, the Communists were gleefully concluding on this matter that we were going back to our old maladroit ways. . . . On the question of public ownership I would urge that we be tolerant and practical and that the test be not ideological preference but the American interest. . . .

That, of course, is the rub. It must be made clear to the American taxpayer precisely what the "American interest" is. To the extent that he thinks of economic aid as mere do-goodism, he will be outraged by any contribution of his tax dollars to a "socialist" enterprise. To the extent that he erroneously equates any degree of public ownership with communism, he feels betrayed by such contributions. Outright opponents of foreign aid have taken no pains to distinguish between "mixed" economies which support democratic government, as in India, and the so-called "socialist" police states of Russia and Red China.

Foreign aid administrators have in a sense abetted their enemies by not being frank enough with the public. Out of an overly nice concern for the sensibilities of recipient countries, our aid too often has been presented as a gesture of unalloyed love—a presentation that might satisfy Ladies' Aid

Societies but is unlikely to command the enthusiasm of the average American trying to rear and educate a family and pay taxes too. Our aid administrators have not succeeded in spelling out to the taxpayer how his "interests" may better be served by controlling his "irritations."

This breakdown in the dialogue between the people who administer our aid program and those who pay for it—the public—has in some respects frustrated the program itself. More straight talk like Galbraith's is needed if the program is to be supported and its ends achieved. Galbraith correctly underscored the impracticability of trying to remake an ancient, caste-ridden, overpopulated, underdeveloped nation like India into a likeness of the comparatively young, prosperous technological society of the United States. Insistence that our own patterns of economic development be rigidly applied in India caused resentment there and denied our aid dollars the propaganda advantage they might have bought. In contrast, the Soviet Union had reaped one of its rare propaganda harvests from having earlier built a public-owned steel plant at Bhilai in Central India.

American congressional reaction to Bokaro typified the paradoxical nature of foreign aid investment and our sometimes self-defeating attitudes toward it. Some of our best investments have been our most "irritating." A dramatic case in point was our aid to Poland and Yugoslavia—particularly Yugoslavia. We not only have given them economic help, but have even provided Yugoslavia's President Tito with quite sophisticated weaponry. Yugoslavia is not, like India, a state that embraces a certain amount of state ownership as a path toward political democracy. It is flat-out, unequivocally Communist.

The argument against aid to Yugoslavia is usually begun by observing that "if war broke out tomorrow Yugoslavia would be in the Soviet camp, using our own weapons against

us." There are two answers to this. This first is that our aid
policy is directed to the prevention of war and assumes that
war would be most likely if the Communist bloc felt strong
and cohesive enough to venture it. Our aid to Yugoslavia,
which had shown considerable independence from Moscow,
was meant to help loosen Moscow's grip on Eastern Europe,
and has done so to a considerable degree. The second answer is that in an all-out war, such arms as we have given
Yugoslavia would not matter much. The nuclear arsenals of
the United States and Russia are sufficient to blow the world
to kingdom come.

During the Stalin era Yugoslavia was a country in which
Moscow-controlled troops menaced the borders of Greece,
Austria, Italy and Albania. Over a fifteen-year period we invested some $2.5 billion in aid to Yugoslavia. Among the po-
litical returns we got were these: Tito withdrew his country
from the Cominform, the Moscow-controlled agency of
worldwide subversion. He withdrew Yugoslav help from the
abortive Communist civil war in Greece. The Yugoslav-
Italian border dispute over Trieste was amicably settled. Tito
refused to join the Moscow-controlled Warsaw Pact of Eastern European nations to counterbalance our NATO.

In the late summer of 1963 Soviet Premier Khrushchev
made a "good will" visit to Yugoslavia, received a cordial
but noncommittal reception, finally got bored and went
home. Tito on a subsequent visit to the Western Hemisphere
carefully avoided any visit to Communist Cuba, which he
knew was an abomination to the United States. By the fall
of 1963 his country was even talking about paying up its
overdue debts to the United Nations where Yugoslavia had
also exhibited independence of Moscow by voting on occasion with the United States or nonaligned nations.

These were not small victories in the cold war for the
United States, which sometimes received much less agree-

able treatment from its "friends." French President Charles de Gaulle, whose country received more United States aid than any other in the world—$9 billion plus—was wont, for instance, to refer to the United States and Britain as "Anglo-Saxon" objects of considerable suspicion. De Gaulle, too, would have no part in financing United Nations operations we felt were necessary to the preservation of peace unless he felt these operations contributed directly to France's mystical and glorious destiny.

The point is simply that we got a big diplomatic "bang for our buck" in Yugoslavia—not despite the fact that it was Communist, but because it was. Yet our irritation with the admittedly unpleasant political fact of Yugoslavian communism led the 87th Congress to cut Yugoslavia off from most-favored-nation treatment at a time when 75 per cent of its trade was with the West. This smacked of throwing away one's winnings—much like a card player who holds a royal flush but tosses in his hand because he doesn't like the color of the cards. Happily, the favored-nation status was restored by Congress in 1963.

There has been a tendency on the part of our administrators and some donee countries to sidestep controversy about American help for local projects through the so-called "nonproject loan." Under these loans American goods can be bought and used for whatever purposes the donee wishes. As a result, the propaganda impact of our aid effort has been diffused and many projects to which we contribute are not readily recognizable as the products of our aid.

Conversely, the American taxpayer is not as aware as he should be of the use to which his money is being put. All he knows is that it has gone. This is in itself an irritating discovery, which will more and more get in the way of his interests until he can be convinced that his money is not being wasted.

9 *The Korea-Formosa Armed Camp*

Eleven hundred years before Christ a peace-loving and inventive people were calling their Far Eastern homeland Chosen, meaning Morning Calm. The name now has an ironic ring. Thousands of Americans died there in an inconclusive war that cost us $18 billion. In addition, we spent more than $3.3 billion in military aid and $2.1 billion in economic aid between 1945 and 1963. The land of Morning Calm is better known as Korea, a Utah-sized, talon-shaped peninsula pointing from the continental underbelly of Red China toward the islands of Japan.

Our heavy investment of blood and cash earned us 136,937 dead and 33,629 wounded in the Korean War. They fell at such bleakly memorable places as Heartbreak Ridge and Porkchop Hill. Militarily, it earned us an uncertain truce, with Korean and Chinese troops poised above the South Korean border to strike if they should find it to their advantage. Economically, South Korea was in trouble despite our aid. Politically, it was ruled by a military dictatorship.

As in so many other areas, we were pulled into this ancient land by the ugly undertow of world power politics. During its long history it had fallen under Chinese and Japanese influence until in the sixteenth century it rid itself of both and was for some three hundred years known as the "Hermit Kingdom." In the late nineteenth century Japan had opened several Korean ports for trade. The United States in 1882 entered into a commercial treaty. Following the 1904–5 Russo-Japanese War the Japanese again began to dominate Korea and in 1910 annexed it, ruling it completely until the end of World War II. That was where we originally came in.

Our then ally, Russia, held Korea as far south as the 38th parallel. We moved into the southern half of the peninsula. The problem of what to do about Korea fell to the newly organized United Nations. The Russians, of course, rejected the United Nations' good offices in the Communist north. A United Nations commission did supervise democratic elections in the south, where a duly elected National Assembly drafted a constitution and elected a longtime fighter for Korean independence and national hero, Syngman Rhee, as President.

Russia announced a pull-out from North Korea by the end of 1948. We pulled out of South Korea by mid-1949. But in June of 1950 the North Korean Communists attacked their southern brethren in an effort to "unify" the country, an act of bald aggression that the United Nations charter had outlawed. Russia, in a fit of politically ill-timed pique, had stalked out of the United Nations the preceding January and was not on hand with her usual *"nyet"* when the world body voted support to South Korea. Outraged and outmaneuvered, the Russians promptly contested the legality of the United Nations decision.

Thus, the Korean War of 1950–53 pitted United States troops, later bolstered by the forces of fifteen other United Nations countries in lesser numbers, against the Russian-supplied troops of North Korea, and, eventually, hordes of Red Chinese "volunteers." It was a seesaw war, eventually brought to its inconclusive close by political decision rather than military might.

Gen. Douglas MacArthur, in command of United Nations forces, favored crossing the Yalu River border of Manchuria to strike at Red Chinese supply lines. President Truman feared that this tactic might expand the Korean "police action" into a global war. The impasse was resolved by Truman's sacking of MacArthur. A truce agreement was finally signed July 27, 1953, and the charade of apparently endless "peace conference" talks began on October 26. As if in celebration of this anniversary, a decade later an armed Communist band crossed the demilitarized zone and gunned down three American soldiers in a jeep, killing two and wounding one.

Against this confused and bloody backdrop, our peacetime aid to Korea fell into much the same sort of economic and political beartrap that it did in South Vietnam. Both countries were inexperienced in self-government, Korea having been run by Japan as South Vietnam had been run by the French. Both economies were shaky from want of development and the drains of war. Each nation had hopefully established its new republic with a strong-man hero at the helm, both of whom wound up running oppressive and unpopular regimes.

A good deal of our aid to Korea was wasted. For instance, organized racketeers in Korea carted off much of the $80 million worth of surplus material we had left there for sale after the war. The auctioned surpluses were meant to help Korean commercial interests by replenishing their stocks at low cost and thereby indirectly bolstering the Korean economy. But Korean gangsters, working behind the façade of a disabled veterans' organization, muscled in, "fixed" bid offerings, strong-armed and drove away legitimate bidders, and then bought surpluses at artificially low prices and resold them at huge profits. It was estimated at the time that the gangster operations were costing the United States $100,-000 a month on small-lot sales. Thus, despite our protests to the Korean government, local thugs were reaping huge profits at the expense of the American taxpayer.

Late in 1961 a survey team of the House Foreign Affairs Committee visited Korea. They reported, "Money saving does not appear to be an important objective in the administration of United States aid, and disregard of rules and procedures by senior officials apparently does not involve any significant penalty . . ."

They found our aid people in Korea "hoarding" millions in unused funds on the off chance they could justify their use later. Meanwhile, these same bureaucrats were eager wherever possible to encourage expenditure of our aid dollars. The team reported:

"When they [the aid administrators] found that United States aid funds programmed to finance the import of commodities into Korea were not being used as fast as anticipated, the United States officials administering economic assistance to Korea approved a system of incentives to Korean importers to speed up United States-financed imports. Greater incentives were given for imports financed by the United States than for imports financed with Korea's own dollars. . . .

"United States officials responsible . . . said it was important to get business going again in order to bring conditions back to normal as soon as possible after the [1961] revolution. Second, it was feared that unless the pipeline of commodities on order was kept filled, a resumption of demand would be followed by shortages, resulting in price increases and disturbed conditions. These arguments have a certain validity, but they would apparently apply as much to the utilization of Korea's own money as United States funds. . . .

"It is normal reaction for responsible officials, after a program has been approved and funds made available to carry it out, to try to carry it out and to regard all impediments and delays as obstacles to be overcome. In this case, the attitude of United States officials was that a falloff in demand for United States-financed imports represented a postponement of necessary expenditure."

In other words, the cardinal sin within the aid bureaucracy is not failure to save money. The sin is failure to spend it. Rather than return it to the Treasury, it may be hoarded for future expenditure. But word must not get around that an administrator had aid money available and was unable to find some excuse for spending it.

The General Accounting Office, however, found that the spending excuse cited did not hold up. In a 1962 report to Congress the GAO said that the $1.2 billion spent by the United States in Korea from 1957 to 1961 had actually stunted economic growth and encouraged corruption. The $200-million-a-year level of aid was "beyond the capacity of the Korean economy to absorb productively or of its government to administer efficiently," the GAO found.

One reason for inefficient administration of our aid by recipient countries is that our own people would rather waste a buck than buck a foreign buddy. The House team, on its swing through Korea, Turkey and Vietnam, came to this conclusion. They reported, "United States officials administering aid programs in foreign countries place great emphasis on the cordiality of their relations with the governments of the countries where they work.

"There is an apparent tendency for United States officials to avoid insisting on compliance with procedures [because they are] annoying to the government with which they work.

Country administrators of the United States aid programs should not be required to follow the rule book regardless of political consequences. Neither should they be permitted to disregard the rules merely to avoid disturbing pleasant relationships."

Other examples of waste uncovered by Congressional investigators and the watchdog General Accounting Office included these:

Item: We turned over to Korea in 1955 the job of distributing our military aid to her own forces. This was at a time when the Koreans, ill-trained for the job to start with, had not even sorted out the mountains of postwar surplus we had left there. Warehouse facilities were bulging and badly located. This invited pilferage of our aid supplies, many of which were consumer-type items in short supply among the civilian population. The invitation to pilfer was widely accepted, although later improvements in supply techniques and firm Korean government action brought improvements.

Item: A team of House investigators found our military services operating in Korea in late 1959 as though they did not know each other: "Flour for the Korean Air Force is separately requisitioned from the United States Air Force stocks in the United States and separately stored in Korea—in spite of the fact that an identical but many times larger operation was being carried on for the Korean Army [by the United States Army]."

Item: Comptroller General Joseph Campbell reported early in 1963 that millions of dollars' worth of our military aid equipment was being wastefully used because the Korean Army would not spend aid funds earmarked to maintain it.

Item: Until 1960 there was no assurance that local currency aid to Korea was spent for the purposes for which it was earmarked, because the Defense Department and our foreign aid agency could not agree on who was supposed to review the program, Campbell reported.

Item: Campbell also reported that in 1961 the Korean Army had overstated its needs for food, clothing and other materials by $4.7 million. GAO auditors said that "Korean Army personnel informed us that cost estimates were generally prepared in excess of what they believed would actually be expended in order to insure adequacy of funds."

Item: In a 1961 report Campbell's investigators found that as a result of bad management "material valued at $2.1 million was on order in excess of requirements" at the U.S. Army Signal Depot at Ascom City, Korea.

Campbell recommended that since the United States was financing 95 per cent of the Korean military budget, it would be better to control operations on a project-by-project basis than to make one lump-sum contribution. The Pentagon rejected this proposal, however, on grounds that it would be "an infringement on the sovereign rights" of South Korea and impose an "impractical" administrative burden. Campbell disagreed and recommended further that aid funds be withheld "when evidence exists that either agreed-upon projects are not being undertaken or earmarked funds are being used for nonapproved purposes."

Obviously in Korea as elsewhere waste and aid were too often bedfellows. But we were fortunate at least that our financial and military underpinning of oppressive South Korean governments had not made the United States the target of popular ill will, as had the oppressions of the Diem regime in South Vietnam. In Korea the "April Revolution" of 1960 had started as a peaceful student demonstration against undemocratic aspects of the regime of aged Syngman Rhee. The students, however, identified the United States more as an inspiration for their protests than an object of their dissatisfactions.

They were protesting such police state tactics as the clos-
ing of an opposition newspaper, an allegedly rigged Vice-
Presidential election won by Rhee's political friend, Lee Ki
Poong, over the incumbent, Dr. John M. Chang of the opposition Democratic party, and the promulgation of undemocratic laws. In demonstrations on April 18–19 nearly 200
students were killed and 7,000 Koreans were injured when
Rhee's police opened fire. The United States moved quickly.
Secretary of State Christian Herter summoned the Korean
Ambassador to his office and told him bluntly that we believed that the demonstrations were "a reflection of popular
dissatisfaction over the conduct of the recent elections and
repressive measures unsuited to a free democracy." Herter
suggested, in short, that the Rhee government shape up.

Following another demonstration April 26, Rhee stepped
down. A caretaker government prosecuted election frauds,
reshuffled the military and cleaned out Rhee's police. The
following July the Democratic party, which had opposed
Rhee, prevailed at the polls. The new assembly named a
British-educated archeologist, Posun Yun, as President. Dr.
Chang, the former Vice-President, became Premier.

The new government, however, lasted less than a year. Dr.
Chang's seeming inability to untangle Korea's knotty eco-
nomic problems led to his overthrow by a military junta on
May 16, 1961. Gen. Chung Hee Park, who emerged as the
junta's strong man, arrested deposed government leaders.
Political activity was banned. The press was controlled.
United States-Korea relations cracked, but did not break,
under the strain. Then they eased considerably after General
Park made a good-will visit to the United States in Novem-
ber of 1961.

Park initiated a five-year plan for industrial development,
sought to improve relations with Japan, and pardoned many
of the nearly 30,000 political prisoners the junta had seized

when it took over. But Park obviously was reluctant to make good on his take-over pledge to return Korea to democratic government by May of 1963. By late 1962 he was angling to keep control by running for President as a civilian, with his twenty-one-man junta running for assembly seats beneath the banner of a junta-organized Democratic Republican party. Under political pressure, he then announced he would not run if the future government would continue the junta's programs and take no reprisals against it. Next he proposed extending military rule for four years.

Finally, yielding to further pressures, Park did schedule elections for October 15, 1963—and immediately began doing his best to rig them. A few weeks before election day he retired from the Army so he could run for President as a civilian. He took charge of the junta-spawned Democratic Republican party and reshuffled it to his own advantage. And he twice jailed his chief critic, a retired lieutenant general, Korean war hero and former premier, Song Yo Chan, who had originally been a member of the Park junta but got out when it became apparent that Park was more interested in personal power than in restoring democracy to Korea.

Despite the elaborate prearrangements, the diminutive (five-feet-four, 141-pound) general-turned-civilian emerged victorious by only a slim margin of 156,026 votes out of 11,036,175 votes cast. His major opponent, Posun Yun, who had served as President during the first ten months after the 1961 coup, might have defeated Park had the anti-junta vote been less diffuse. But withdrawal from the race of Song Yo Chan and a former Premier, Huh Chung, resulted in the voiding of some 950,000 votes. Ballots cast for candidates of the Right Citizens League, the Autumn Breeze Society and the New Prosperity party siphoned off another 830,000 votes and gave Park his victory. He had won with only some 45 per cent of the popular vote.

It was, nevertheless, a genuine victory for Park. He had carried out, albeit under pressure, his pledge to hold free elections. They were, it was agreed, the freest and most peaceably conducted in the young republic's history. Indirectly, Park's narrow victory was also something of a diplomatic plus for the United States policy of seeking to encourage constitutional, civilian government, as opposed to junta rule.

Park had been compelled to present himself as a civilian candidate and campaign on a pledge of orderly transition to civilian rule under a new constitution that gave the President power to dominate a new one-chamber legislature. The close contest served notice that a majority of the electorate felt that Korea's serious problems were amenable to democratic solution. It did not, however, insure domestic tranquillity. Several days after election, South Korean police arrested thirty anti-government university students and charged them with plotting to seize key government buildings. Government and opposition parties accused each other of election malpractices, and government prosecutors were instructed to prepare cases against 270 persons, including Yun. The continuing influence of such key junta powers as Kim Chong Pil, former Central Intelligence Agency chief who had helped plot the 1961 coup and organize the Democratic Republican party, left the future of democratic government cloudy.

Park himself personified the political confusions and shifting allegiances with which the United States had to deal in trying to bring some stability to Southeast Asia. The chain-smoking, thrice-married Park was born of a family of well-to-do landowners in 1916 near Taegu in southern Korea at a time when Japan controlled the country. A graduate of a Japanese military academy in Manchuria, he served as an officer in the Japanese Army in World War II. After the war he was also graduated from a Korean Academy organized by the United States Army and became a captain in the Korean constabulary. A year later he was charged with Communist intrigue and court-martialed—a charge that cost him votes in the 1963 elections. At the time of the 1961 coup he was back in the Army with the rank of major general. He gave himself four stars when he took over the government. The United States could only cross its fingers and hope that as a civilian President Park might prove to be something more than a military dictator in disguise.

Dealing with Far Eastern military dictators, however, was hardly anything new for the United States. The daddy of them all was our Chinese friend, Generalissimo Chiang Kai-shek, President of the exiled Nationalist Chinese government on the island of Formosa. Chiang nourished himself with dreams of one day returning to the mainland. We nourished Chiang with some $4.5 billion in economic and military aid.

Chiang and his Kuomintang party were driven into exile by Mao Tse-tung and the Communists in 1949. The Kuomintang had overthrown the feudal Manchu dynasty in 1912. Chiang, a disciple of revolutionary leader Sun Yat-sen, had been trained in part in Russia. But in 1926, a year after the death of Sun, Chiang took over control of the Nationalist army, kicked the Communists out of government, subdued the northern Chinese warlords and unified China under his government.

The 1937 Japanese attack on China forced Chiang into common cause with the Communists, but he remained in control as Generalissimo of the Chinese forces. He was our valued and valorous ally throughout World War II. His contributions to Allied victory in the Orient were epic. But with Japan obviously near defeat the Chinese Communists began turning their attention to Chiang's downfall. Chiang countered with adoption of a new constitution and the holding of popular elections. The Communist drive, however, was bolstered by popular dissatisfaction with the corruption and repressions that had characterized the Kuomintang, and Chiang was driven onto Formosa.

Although our aid investment in Chiang's island fortress was huge, it also yielded valuable returns, giving us a strategic base of operations only some 100 miles from the Chinese mainland. Nor did the Formosans suffer in a material sense from the invasion of Chiang and his minions. As a result of our aid to Chiang's government, they ate better, dressed better and lived better.

With the help of American advisers, for instance, a land reform plan was instituted. When Chiang fled to the island, only one-fourth of all Formosan farmers owned their own land and many were paying rents amounting to 70 per cent of their crop. As a result of reforms, rents were cut to a maximum of 37.5 per cent and the number of farmers who owned their land jumped within a decade from about 210,000 to 470,000. Over a ten-year period agricultural output climbed 40 per cent and industrial production was up 180 per cent, although many of the gains were siphoned off in increased taxes to support Chiang's military machinery.

Here again, however, a hard-eyed look at our aid disclosed some familiar patterns of waste. House investigators visiting Formosa in late 1959, for instance, found that equipment specially designed for a "monumental" fertilizer plant we were building on the island was inadequate, new equipment would be needed, and that costs would climb substantially over estimates.

More than half of our aid to Formosa was military. The General Accounting Office in 1961 sent investigators to see what had happened to some of the Army equipment we sent there. They found that "a substantial portion of equipment furnished under the military assistance program had become defective because of inadequate maintenance and poor supply support." Inspection of four Formosan divisions revealed that "large numbers of tanks and vehicles . . . [and] large quantities of engineering equipment were inoperative, and much of the signal equipment required additional maintenance. Other items of a classified nature had also deteriorated. In consequence, attainment of the objectives of the United States under the Military Assistance Program had been adversely affected. . . . It is apparent that substantial quantities of equipment were delivered over and above that which could be maintained and utilized."

In a report to Congress in late summer of 1962 the GAO also had this to say about maintenance and supply of the billions of dollars' worth of equipment we had sent to Formosa, Korea and other Far Eastern countries:

". . . In one country almost one-fifth of the tanks delivered under the Military Assistance Program were unserviceable or [inoperative] as of October 31, 1960. In another instance, a technical inspection by country personnel disclosed that about a third of the 1100 vehicles in two divisions were considered to be unserviceable and in no condition for a planned field maneuver.

"Our reviews also disclosed, on the basis of a test conducted by technicians in one country at our request, that about 38 per cent of the radio communication equipment had an effective range of only one-third to two-thirds of that for which it was designed.

"Another indication of the magnitude of the lack of maintenance which permitted deterioration to the point where vehicles were not economically repairable is the fact that in one country over 29,000 combat-support vehicles were scrapped in a four-and-a-half-year period ended December 31, 1960. This was considerably in excess of that which could be reasonably expected through normal attrition. The unsatisfactory maintenance of equipment furnished under the Military Assistance Program in these countries has, as a consequence, adversely affected the attainment of United States objectives. . . ."

The GAO conceded that our military people faced staggering problems in attempting to supply comparatively new armies. The language barrier, high personnel turnover, widespread illiteracy and casual attitudes toward efficiency and economy in these armies presented heavy handicaps.

Yet, the GAO found, "there are many areas in which the military assistance advisory groups could have and should have exerted more action" to cut down on such vast waste.

Meanwhile, Chiang's United States-supported regime on Formosa, not unlike his earlier mainland regime, was anything but a model of popularly responsible government. Albert Axelbank, who for nearly two years until mid-1962 was bureau manager for United Press International on Formosa, wrote in the September, 1963, issue of *Harper's Magazine:*

Behind the mask of a benevolent, freedom-loving Chinese Nationalist government on Formosa, there exists today an unpopular, elite party dictatorship that rules the island with an iron hand. In the guise of "Mobilization for Counter-attack Against Communist China," the regime of Generalissimo Chiang Kai-shek has trampled upon basic human rights and stifled free political expression. Under the cloak of "national emergency," it has waged a campaign of police terror. As a result, Chiang's Kuomintang government has alienated the overwhelming majority of Formosa's native-born citizens, who comprise 80 per cent of the island's 11 million people.

Formosans were allowed only the tiniest of representation in the Chiang government. Fewer than 40 were in the 1,500-member National Assembly, the body charged with electing the President and Vice-President and amending the constitution. Only a handful of Formosans were in the 500-member Parliament. In the Cabinet only the Minister of Interior was a Formosan. Although Formosans provided more than 75 per cent of the ground troops in Chiang's Army, practically all of the nearly 1,000 generals and admirals were Chinese.

Indeed two of the generals were Chiang's sons. The eldest, Gen. Chiang Ching-kuo, who attended the Soviet Military and Political Institute as a youth, controlled the secret police. The youngest, Chiang Wego, was a general in command of the Army's armored corps. Other top generals were inner-circle members of the Kuomintang party.

The Chiang government had rigged local elections, stuffed ballot boxes, "bloc-voted" Nationalist soldiers, exercised tight control over Formosa's provincial government, and suppressed opposition parties. In the summer of 1960 a group of business and political leaders sought to form a new party, the China Democrats. Chiang's Formosa Garrison Command arrested one of its leaders, a mainlander and former Kuomintang member named Lei Chen, charged him with sedition and harboring a Communist agent, and at a one-day military court-martial sentenced him to ten years in prison. A second leader was arrested the same day and charged with fraud in a housing deal. And simultaneously, a third leader, Henry Kao, who had once been mayor of Taipeh, was charged with malpractice and burglary during his term of office. Under the pretext of promoting the national security, the Chiang government has also gagged independent newspapers and magazines.

The Chiang regime was so unpopular, in fact, that there were Formosan exiles in Japan, awaiting return to an "independent" Formosa, just as Chiang waited hopefully on the island for an opportunity to return to the mainland. Dr. Thomas Wen-i Liao, who held a doctorate in chemical engineering from Ohio State University, was President of a "Provisional Government of the Republic of Formosa," duly elected by some 1,000 of his exile followers in Japan.

Sentiment on the island for independence was overwhelming, and our support of the oppressive Chiang regime cost us friends. We could not, of course, desert Chiang. But we could, as Axelbank urged in his report, "insist that the Nationalists wipe out . . . the terror on the island and allow the Formosans some of the democratic freedoms we claim to uphold and defend."

One of the legislators least impressed with our investment in Korea and Formosa was Senate Foreign Relations Committeeman Wayne Morse of Oregon, who tried unsuccessfully to reduce aid to the two countries. Rasped Morse:

"The Taiwan [Formosan] Army has more generals, who are receiving big, fat pay, than the total number of generals in all of our military establishment. . . . We had better take a look at some of the featherbedding we are supporting in various countries. . . .

"I am not frightened by the bugaboo argument that if we do not support Taiwan and the South Koreans, the Communists will take over. We have our own army in South Korea and our fleet protecting Taiwan from invasion. . . . In my judgment, the military aid we have been giving Taiwan will be worthless if we ever get into a military combat with Red China. . . .

"Taiwan . . . is often considered a showcase of what aid can do to raise living standards and productivity; but in terms of what we have spent, I do not believe the results have been so remarkable. Moreover, political freedom for the seven million or so Taiwanese whom we delivered to the Chiang regime seems as remote as ever. . . . The United States in effect imposed him upon them as a puppet, and has been supporting him ever since; and it is about time for us to withdraw at least part of this drain on the American tax-payers."

One thing was certain from our aid experiences in South Korea and Nationalist China. Our lavish outpourings of aid had achieved only limited, although significant, objectives. We had bought bases of operation in strategically vital areas. They came complete with armed nationals ready to battle our mutual Communist enemies and thus cut down the need for or size of commitments of our own troops. We had bought a strong hand with which to play the international game of power politics, which we, as a world power, had to play to survive. To the extent that our economic and military aid was inefficiently administered, as it was in some instances, it represented a degree of economic waste. But the goals were politically justified over the short haul. We got something for our money.

Only history will tell whether over the long haul we invested wisely. We were readily identified with regimes that were, at worst, repressive, and, at best, something less than what we recognize as popularly responsible and responsive governments. They were just about all we had to work with at the time. We could and should have done more to make them popularly responsive. To the extent that we did not, this, too, was waste not only of our present investment but of the long-term dividends which we hoped it might produce.

10 *Mr. Nasser and His Neighbors*

You name it—and jolly Uncle Sam has been there with his bag of foreign aid goodies. From A (Afghanistan) to Z (Zanzibar). Some of the strangest among many strange places he chose to distribute his largesse were to be found in the Near East and Africa. Try Jordan as an example.

It was not even a nation until after World War II. And it would not have remained one long if our aid had not kept it glued together. The less than 40,000-square-mile Near Eastern Hashemite Kingdom, over 75 per cent desert, was watered with what the State Department likes to refer to as "budget support." This means that we underwrote the Jordanian government. Our aid amounted to more per year than the Jordanian government could collect from its own sources, mostly customs duties and excise taxes. Thus, in 1962 our contribution was $62.6 million compared to the $52.5 million the Jordanian government managed to raise.

Through 1963 we had spent nearly $415 million in Jordan, and the prospects for our continued spending in the arid little Arab kingdom were excellent. Asked during House hearings on the fiscal 1964 foreign aid money bill if Jordan would ever be able to get off the dole, Assistant AID Administrator William S. Gaud candidly replied:

"I think it is unlikely that they will. They have plans under way, and we are helping them. If their plan works out, they hope to get along without budget support by 1970. I personally think that is overoptimistic."

Meanwhile we were irrigating arid Jordanian land at a cost of some $700 per acre, providing health and technical services to farmers, helping build up a Jordanian tourist industry, educating schoolboys, building roads, etc. But at least Jordan's King Hussein was pro-West. Not so the United Arab Republic's Gamal Abdel Nasser who, fired by dreams of heading a Pan-Arab union, was wont to turn his government-controlled press and radio loose for mad-dog attacks on the United States and our European partners.

Yet through fiscal 1963 Nasser's domain had received $807 million in United States aid. Nasser was furious when we refused to build his Aswan Dam for him, but there was also evidence that we had "got to" him with our other aid gifts. Despite nicey-nicey disclaimers from our diplomats, we had bribed him into being somewhat more reasonable. During hearings on the 1964 budget Democratic Representative George W. Andrews of Alabama led Assistant Secretary of State Phillips Talbot onto the subject this way:

Andrews: "You state the United States' objective is a stable and neutral United Arab Republic amicable to Western interests as the best guarantee of stability in the Near East and the survival of the smaller states in the area, including Israel."

Talbot: "Yes, sir."

Andrews: "Those countries are bitter enemies, are they not?"

Talbot: "There is a lot of stress and strain in the Near East as there has been for some time."

Andrews: "Have we secured from the Egyptian government officials any kind of guarantee that they will not oppress
Israel in any way?"

Talbot: "No, sir, we have not."

Andrews: "Have we guaranteed in our aid to Egypt the
security of Israel?"

Talbot: "This is an area very hard to document. I would
say the stresses between Egypt and Israel were greater when
there was no aid program to the United Arab Republic than
they have been in the last several years."

Andrews: "Is this aid in any way a bribe to keep them
from oppressing against Israel?"

Talbot: "No, sir: I would not describe it as a bribe. I would
say the United Arab Republic was by far the largest country
in the whole area. It is doing a good deal on its domestic
front in development and it is in our interest that it should
focus even more on development. . . . There seems to us to
have been some change in United Arab Republic attitudes
with respect, for example, to nuclear testing where they stood
against the Soviet resumption of tests, with respect to economic development where they have taken quite a balanced
line as compared with the line that they had taken somewhat
earlier, vis-à-vis the Western countries. On the broader front
I think one can see a number of changes."

There then followed a colloquy in which all parties
seemed to agree that the Soviets' heavy-handed attempts to
move into the Near East had backfired, and that Nasser's
more reasonable attitude was attributable at least in part to
this fact. Republican Representative Gerald R. Ford, Jr.,
of Michigan got back on the pay-off tack by eliciting testimony from Assistant AID Administrator Gaud that we had
given Nasser's Egypt $49.2 million in 1959, $92.9 million in
1960, $106.4 million in 1961, $224.1 million in 1962 and $195
million in 1963.

Commented Ford, "The increase since 1959 could lead someone to the conclusion that we have been able to talk with the United Arab Republic beginning with the mid-fifties to the present time, primarily because of the increase in our financial support. Is that a fair analysis?"

"Pretty expensive talk, indeed," commented Democratic Representative Joseph M. Montoya of New Mexico. Asked Democratic Representative J. Vaughan Gary of Virginia, "It looks like money has been doing most of the talking, has it not?"

Admitted Talbot, "I think the aid is an important part of moving the United Arab Republic into a broader relationship with the West than it had had and thereby moving it rather away from the U.S.S.R. I think this has been an important factor in it; yes, sir."

Asked Democratic Representative Otto Passman of Louisiana, "Is it a matter of talk is cheap, but it takes money to try to buy so-called friends?"

"Well, sir," replied Talbot, "it is not a question of buying friends. It is a question of getting the largest country in the Near East into a posture which is healthier for our interests than the posture in which it was in the 1956 to 1958 period. . . . We have, I think, in this program, helped to bring about a situation in the Near East in which our interests are better protected than they were . . . when, you will recall, the Suez Canal was nationalized; Arab-Israel hostility was greatly intensified; the Iraq Petroleum Pipeline Company was destroyed. . . ."

All of which would seem to indicate that Mr. Talbot might as well have answered Representative Andrews' question about our Egyptian investment's being "in any way a bribe" with a succinct "Yes." And if the money really was buying more protection of our interests, which is the basic purpose of foreign aid as a diplomatic tool, it would little matter what the "gift" was called.

A majority of the Congress, however, doubted that aid to Nasser really was serving our interests. Both houses adopted amendments, pointed squarely at Nasser, which would deny aid to countries which wage aggressive war. Senator Ernest Gruening, a liberal Democrat from Alaska, made the case this way in Senate debate November 7, 1963:

"A year ago last September, Russian Ilyushin planes were waiting to carry a large contingent of Gamal Abdel Nasser's troops into Yemen. This troop movement coincided with the announcement of a revolt in Yemen. Since that time, Nasser has kept 28,000 troops there, making war on the people of Yemen, at a cost of $500,000 a day. This figure was vouched for by our military attaché in Cairo. . . .

"In other words, while our money is designed to help the poor people of Egypt—those who are undernourished, under-housed and underclothed—the money intended for their benefit is being spent on aggressive warfare elsewhere.

"This is only one of the many moves that Nasser is making to dominate the Middle East. When we visited there, we were informed by the military attachés that their movements . . . were severely restricted. They could move only a few blocks from the Embassy or from their location. But the Russian technicians, the Russian military, were allowed to go everywhere. Indeed, they were supplying Nasser with all his arms. So, at the same time while Nasser has Russian equipment, Russian technicians and ex-Nazi technicians, we —the United States—pour money in Egypt. Nasser is making war with our dollars just as though we were paying for his military adventures.

"Within the past week, Egyptian troops have moved into Algeria, to help Algeria in its war on Morocco, in consequence of which the King of Morocco has severed relations with Algeria. Last week there were riots in Lebanon; each day, some Middle East country is agitated and stirred up by Nasser. Nasser has never ceased to declare his intention to invade Israel and drive the Israelis into the sea.

"His broadcasts nightly, beamed over the Cairo radio, to the operation of which we unfortunately contributed, beam hatred and preach assassination of rulers of countries Nasser wishes to destroy. He has preached assassination of the King of Jordan [and] the leaders of Lebanon [and] . . . others. I believe it is time that our aid, under those circumstances, should stop. . . .

"It is depressing to think our policies are promoting aggressive war in the Middle East. It not only permits countries to use our aid for aggressive warfare, but it causes nations such as Jordan and Israel to fear for their lives and increase their arms. So we are in effect stimulating competition in war in the Middle East. We are, indeed, promoting an arms race. How inconsistent is the practical effect of our blind policy of financing Nasser with our professions of wanting a world of peace."

The Near East did indeed present a bizarre field for our aid investment. One of the beneficiaries of our assistance, for example, was oil-rich Saudi Arabia's King Saud, who drew down $44 million a year from his government's treasury for expenses and had a private fortune estimated at $100 million. His Majesty, who ruled his tribal people with an iron whim, had enjoyed a long and lusty life during which he had wed and discarded hundreds of wives, sired countless offspring, and accumulated only a slightly lesser number of air-conditioned Cadillacs and palaces. His habit of siring princes, who in turn sired more princes, was something of a drain on the treasury. Many of the royal horde had their own palaces. And at last count there were about a thousand princes drawing down a government allowance. But Saudi Arabia was strategically important, and over the years we had given it some $46 million in aid—a comparatively modest amount. It was, in fact, just about equal to the personal bank debts the fruitful princes had piled up.

Elsewhere through 1963 we had dumped more than $3.5 billion into Greece, $4.1 billion into Turkey, $1.4 billion into Iran—all strongly allied with the West, all contributing to the United States goal of containing Communist expansion through the Mediterranean, the Persian Gulf and the Arab world, and all making some degree of domestic socio-political progress. Somewhat less stable beneficiaries included such as oil-rich Iraq ($69 million). During House appropriations hearings Chairman Passman of the Foreign Aid subcommittee asked acidly:

"There have been no new governments [in Iraq] within the last few hours?"

Replied Assistant AID Administrator Gaud, "Not since I left my office."

But AID officials made a strong argument that our aid had provided us a continuing entree into the affairs of this and other essentially unstable societies that communism sought to exploit. It will remain, perhaps, for history to say whether these expenditures were wasteful folly or diplomatic economies. The folly argument was dramatically propounded by Passman as his subcommittee questioned AID Director David Bell. Passman quoted from a news report as follows:

"It is a gloomy moment in history. Not for many years—not in the lifetime of most men who read this paper—has there been so much grave apprehension; never has the future seemed so incalculable as at this time. . . . In France, the political cauldron seethes and bubbles with uncertainty; Russia hangs, as usual, like a cloud, dark and silent upon the horizon of Europe; while all the energies, resources and influences of the British Empire are sorely tried. . . . It is a solemn moment, and no man can feel an indifference—which, happily, no man pretends to feel in the issue of events. Of our own troubles no man can see the end."

Passman asked Bell, "Would that report sound about like the times we are in today?"

Bell: "The times are difficult, and we are all sorely tried, not only the British but we ourselves."

Passman: "You would have to admit that in France the political cauldron seethes and bubbles."

Bell: "Mr. de Gaulle is securely in position at the moment. The future in France is somewhat uncertain."

Passman: " 'Russia hangs, as usual, like a cloud, dark and silent upon the horizon of Europe.' I do not suppose we could discount that too much."

Bell: "Did it mention Communist China?"

Passman: "No. What I read . . . was an excerpt from an article published in *Harper's Weekly*, Volume 1, page 642, October 10, 1857—106 years ago. It points up the idea that the problems we are confronted with today are just about the same type as they were long before we were born.

"Many of the troubles we are confronted with are nothing new. However, it looks as if we are going to go busted trying to cure ills that were here years ago."

Indeed, it seemed that in some emerging nations the ills of poverty and ignorance and disease would require all the wealth of the world—and more—to bring them up to what, by Western standards, would be a minimal level of socio-economic well-being and political viability. This was largely true of Africa. More than thirty nations, in addition to French, British and Portuguese territories, were on our aid list.

Eighty-five per cent of the continent was illiterate. The African's average annual income was $130. There was only one physician for every 17,000 persons—one twenty-fifth the

United States ratio. Most Africans farmed, but the African could produce only about 4 per cent of what his North American counterpart could. Yet, paradoxically, it was a continent of fabulous natural wealth. More than 90 per cent of the diamonds in the world came from Africa. It produced nearly three-fourths of the free world's cobalt, 60 per cent of the gold, half of the chrome and manganese, a fifth of the uranium and asbestos and a fourth of the copper. And its vast treasures had barely been tapped.

Politically, the once "Dark Continent" had fairly blazed onto the international scene. When the United Nations was founded in 1945 it had only four African members—Egypt, Ethiopia, Liberia and South Africa. By late 1963 there were thirty-three African members, nearly a third of the UN's total membership and a larger number of members than that of any other continent. And, contrary to early Western fears, the emerging African nations were not "sitting ducks" for Communist subversion. Having shucked Western colonialism, by and large they were wary of or downright hostile to attempts by the Soviet bloc to subvert their new-found independence. Thus, during the 1962 Cuban crisis, many African votes were cast in the UN on the side of moderation. Other African votes combined to repel Red China's bid for a seat in the world assembly. Although some of the new African countries, like Ghana, seemed to be "nonaligned" in favor of Moscow and against the West, the West had enjoyed some clear diplomatic victories.

Africa, in short, presented a complex but vastly important question. How should the United States preserve its interests in the new nations of the awakening continent? Trying to finance its overnight conversion from the Stone Age culture that prevailed in some areas to American middle-class prosperity would be madness. Ignoring Africa's vast economic and political potential would also be folly. The Presidential Clay committee viewed Africa this way:

"As we consider the African nations, immediate security interests are less evident than in countries adjacent to the Communist bloc. The U.S. does have a stake in helping to create a climate of stability and growth in freedom, however, and the Communists have already displayed their interest and subversive potential in this area. Also, the new countries of Africa in most cases have maintained close ties with the former metropoles [former European colonial powers] without impairment of their full independence, and the latter in turn have displayed considerable willingness to help meet the assistance needs of these young nations. The committee regards Africa as an area where the Western European countries should logically bear most of the necessary aid burden. In fact, this is proving to be the case. . . .

"It can always be said that in fragile, new, developing countries, the United States must provide aid lest they accept it from Communist nations with resulting political penetration and eventual subversion. We cannot accept this view. We believe these new countries value their independence and do not wish to acquire a new master in place of the old one. There already have been instances on the continent to corroborate this belief. While our aid programs in this area are generally new, experience has shown they tend to increase. In the light of its other responsibilities, the United States cannot undertake to support all of the African countries, especially when their ties with other free world nations are largely elsewhere."

Somalia was an example of an area where the Communists had "displayed their interest." By late 1963 the impoverished little republic on the Horn of Africa was, in fact, being treated to a veritable Red fireworks display of interest. Both Russia and Communist China, then engaged in a loud propa-

ganda game of dialectical fratricide, made the 262,000-
square-mile Moslem republic the center of an aid war. Somalia, composed of former British and Italian colonies, had
achieved its independence in 1960. Moscow rushed in with
a $40 million aid program. The Red Chinese countered with
an agreement to cover a $2.8 million Somali budget deficit
and make a $20 million interest-free loan. Chinese tech-
nicians swarmed in, and Red China had the largest embassy
in the Somali capital of Mogadishu.

The Somalis had encouraged Red-bloc help after express-
ing their dissatisfaction with Western aid. The British and
Italian "metropoles" obviously had not come through as the
Clay committee would have hoped. Our commitment to Somalia for fiscal 1963 had amounted to $9.2 million. Why did
we not leave Western aid entirely up to the metropoles?
AID officials supplied this answer, not only to Somalia but to
other African nations: The governments of the new nations
were subject to severe internal pressures from ultranationalist
elements who felt a too-close identification with the nation's
former metropole represented a kind of "neo-colonialism."
By offering our own aid, we gave the new nation an alternative source of assistance. They could then accept aid more
readily from the metropoles.

The popular acceptance of this argument, however, was
considerably weakened by such as Kwame Nkrumah, President (a euphemism for strong man) of Ghana, another former
British colony which achieved independence March 6, 1957.
Nkrumah, like Nasser of Egypt, had grand ideas. His was
a Pan-African federation, with Kwame Nkrumah at its head.
Like Nasser, he also played both sides of the aid street.

He tapped the Red bloc for $69 million in 1961 and an-
other $107 million in 1962. The United States, on the other
hand, was working to wean Nkrumah away from the idea
that state socialism was the key to the former Gold Coast

colony's future. (Although he was educated in the United States, the democratic ideal seemed to have eluded him. He was notoriously ungentle about suppressing opposition to his regime at home, and raucous in his criticism of the West.)

Nevertheless, we had spent some $160 million in aid money in Ghana through 1963 and capped this by arranging to finance a $360 million complex, composed of a dam, power facilities and an aluminum smelter on Ghana's Volta River. Questioned during hearings on the fiscal 1964 aid budget, Edmond C. Hutchinson, Assistant AID Administrator, said our Volta Dam commitment included an escape clause "in the event of the occurrence of extraordinary circumstances."

Said Representative Montoya, "I cannot conceive of a government-owned press [Ghana's] attacking the United States on almost every action we take within the country as not being such an extraordinary situation as to warrant the cancellation of this commitment. . . .

"The sentiment of the American people [is] against making this kind of a loan to Ghana, a country which has indicated an inimical attitude toward the United States. It has oriented its government toward the Soviet bloc, it has indulged in many activities which subvert the welfare of the United States within that country in its international dealings, and I might add further that Ghana has received extensive aid from Russia. I cannot conceive how this project could be of any diplomatic advantage, or any other constructive advantage to the United States, in view of the circumstances surrounding the international decorum of Ghana. . . .

"We in the Congress have to go back to our people and explain why these things are being done. I cannot be convinced that this was a worthwhile investment by the United States. If there were any way in my power I could remove this commitment on the part of the United States, I would surely do it. It is not helping our country, and it is certainly not helping us justify what contribution we make to foreign aid."

Replied Hutchinson, "First, I certainly sympathize with the problem you have with your constituents. This was a close decision. There is no question about it. I also agree with you that the existence of the commitment, and the existence of the loan, is not helping us in the foreign aid program in the sense of our appearance before the Congress and the appropriations we get from the Congress. There is no question about that. That is the truth. But I cannot agree with you that the commitment was not in the interests of the United States. I think it was. . . . I wish we could convince you of the same thing."

The problem with the whole aid program, of course, was that both Congress and the American public were getting harder and harder to convince—even about programs in Africa where the need was obviously greatest and our aid commitment had been comparatively small. Since World War II and through 1963 we had extended only $2.4 billion to the whole continent. On one tour made by Senate Foreign Relations Committeeman Vance Hartke of Indiana, however, the Senator found that even what we were spending was not always prudently used. He criticized "the somewhat frightened attitude of many of our foreign aid Missions toward unreasonable demands on the part of African leaders."

"Too often our Mission directors have acquiesced in projects which bear no relation whatever to the purposes for which foreign aid was established," Hartke reported. "Projects should be refused and no money spent at all rather than begun at the whims of local politicians."

Hartke also found "needless overprogramming of projects," United States military personnel being used to build roads and other AID projects, a "rather topheavy [AID] bureaucracy in many countries out of all proportion to the number of actual workers in the field" and a "tendency for foreign aid workers to live in communities quite far from their . . . projects."

The Senator recommended a much more realistic approach toward our African aid commitments. "Often such aid could be offered on a take-it-or-leave-it basis," he said. "Grants or loans on our part still derive from the money paid as taxes by our own people. I think all foreign aid personnel should be made acutely aware of their responsibilities to the American taxpayer. And I, for one, would rather have foreign aid curtailed than have money needlessly wasted."

So would most of Hartke's colleagues in Congress, as AID officials discovered. Their reception at Congressional budget hearings got cooler and cooler as the results—or lack of them —from our aid efforts became better and better known by more and more legislators. The legislators' instincts, born of political wariness, were to appropriate less and less money. For the Near East, Africa, or anywhere else.

11 *The Soviet "Giveaway"*

United States administration of its foreign aid program over the years has been fraught with well-documented blunders and boondoggles. But it has survived in part because of a popular fear that if we withdrew our dollars, Russian rubles would rush in to fill the politico-economic vacuum and all would be lost. The record dispels this terror, if, indeed, it can be so described.

We are the modern-day creators of cash as a backstop to foreign policy. Our aid efforts, having passed the $100 billion mark, vastly overshadow Red offerings in volume and at least more than match it in effectiveness. The shifty Soviets do not make their contributions to the establishment of a brave new socialist world altogether known. But the best evidence is that they have contributed only a fraction of the aid we have given—and have extended it on much harder terms.

A good deal of Soviet "aid" is figured in terms of technical assistance rather than offers of machinery and equipment. Their loans generally carry interest rates of 2 per cent or a bit higher. This contrasts with our program, which has been made up in greater part of either outright gifts or loans so soft that the fraction-of-1-per-cent-interest rate is hardly enough to cover service costs.

In March of 1963, the best estimate was that Russia had put up less than $12 billion in foreign aid since World War II. Immediately after the war, of course, ravaged Mother Russia was in no position to help anybody except herself. The Soviet aid effort really began about 1954 and was largely directed toward helping Communist-bloc colleagues. Communist-bloc countries have received about $6.2 billion. Loans and grants to non-Communist countries came to some $3.6 billion. Military aid accounted for $2 billion.

By 1963, however, the Russians were becoming even more close-mouthed about their aid offerings. Many of their investments abroad had gone sour. Some were downright disasters. Although Red aid was much more modest than the United States program, it was derived from a much less viable economy. With growing Kremlin concern for bettering the average Russian's standard of living, Khrushchev and Company were apparently reassessing the cost—in both rubles and political results—of competing with Uncle Sam in the hand-out race.

Russian economists were frank to say that Soviet growth rates were not as high as the United States estimated them to be. The Kremlin was urging greater production from farm and factory, neither of which approached the efficiency of their United States counterparts. Meanwhile, abroad the Kremlin was cursed with its own South Vietnam—Cuba. It was awfully strategic, but awfully expensive.

Like America's high-priced President Diem in South Vietnam, Cuba's costly Castro was a questionable Soviet ally, vacillating between cooperation with Russia's coexistence approach to victory for world Communism and the dangerous jingoism of Red China, which insisted that America's nuclear arsenal was only a "paper tiger." Castro would have col-

lapsed without Russian aid. But the $1 million-a-day cost
of propping him up and using his island as a base for Communist infiltration of South America was high for a country
where simple clothing purchases by the average middle-class
Russian required considerable family preplanning.

At the same time and much closer home, the Kremlin was
cursed with another bearded and costly incompetent, Walter
Ulbricht of East Germany. That sad country's supine economy was the real "bone in the throat" Khrushchev gagged on
whenever free, prosperous, capitalist West Berlin was offered
in comparison.

Russia apparently decided it had to cut back somewhere.
The United Nations in 1962 estimated that Soviet economic
aid to underdeveloped countries had been slashed more than
half over a year, down from $680 million in 1960 to $304
million in 1961. But in all likelihood the drop was attributable to more than the disappearance of Russian rubles in
such bottomless pits as Cuba and East Germany. The Soviets
had also been getting little or no political return on their aid
investments in the so-called "uncommitted" countries, many
of which had been eager for aid but downright hostile to
Communist subversion. Other countries had got used to more
liberal American aid, including gifts or loans of equipment
infinitely superior in quality and performance to the shoddy
stuff that Russia was peddling.

Africa provides a dramatic example of an area where
Soviet aid would seem to have had a ready-made market for
political exploitation. Emerging nations, newly free of colonial administration by European powers, tended leftward.
But the Soviets have made little headway in their aid efforts
for several reasons. One is that by long habit Africa looked
to the West for both political formulas and economic help.
The other is that Soviet offerings of some half a million dollars a year are overwhelmed by the combined aid efforts of

the United States (about $4 million annually) and the various European powers that still have a vital stake in the African continent. A third is that the Russians, eager for a quick political return on their investment, apparently have had neither the patience nor the means to provide the kind of massive aid the emerging countries were led to expect.

Guinea, the former French West African territory which became officially independent in 1958, was a case in point. The Communists put on a big aid push. Over a period of nine years they had poured the equivalent of $127 million in grants and credits into the little (106,200 square miles, 2,507,000 population) nation. This was eight and a half times the $15 million that the United States had contributed to Guinea over the same period. But the Communists wanted Africa to see in Guinea what their aid could do. The demonstration backfired.

Premier Sékou Touré, who had been encouraged by the Reds to break with France, signed barter deals with Russia, East Germany, Poland, Czechoslovakia and Communist China. But poorly packaged Russian cement hardened on the docks of Guinea's capital of Conakry during a rainstorm. The Russians declined to buy Guinean bananas that the Soviets' own faulty shipping schedules had left to rot on Conakry's wharfs. East German technicians came in to set up a printing plant that was to grind out Communist propaganda for all of Africa. It never produced at more than 10 per cent of capacity, and the Guinea government opened negotiations with a New York publishing outfit to take it over for the publication of textbooks.

In 1961 Guinea ordered the Soviet Ambassador out of the country, charging that he was conspiring with French Communists to overthrow Touré and install a pro-Communist government. Communist teachers were also given the boot. They were replaced by French nationals and United States

Peace Corpsmen. The ultimate blow to Red prestige was the training in Seattle of Guinean pilots to fly and service United States aircraft that would base at the Soviet-built, Soviet-equipped airport at Conakry. The craft, DC-4s and Lockheed 60s, were secured under contract with Alaskan Airways.

Indonesia, one of the countries that Russia has wooed most ardently, also learned that Communist aid was not the wondrous thing it was cracked up to be. Sometimes it was just cracked. Soviet-built helicopters burned out after 300 flying hours. President Sukarno refused to use one given him by Nikita Khrushchev. He flew only in an American-built chopper. A sugar mill shipped from East Germany worked fine for beet sugar—but not for the cane sugar they grow in Indonesia. Russian-bought submarines were not equipped with the air conditioning needed in tropical Indonesia. Some 2,000 crates of spare parts for Soviet bombers Indonesia had bought showed up one day—with the bills of lading all in Russian, a language Indonesians can't read. The Czechs shipped machinery to build a cement plant into a port where there were no cranes to unload it.

In all, the Soviet Union, its satellites and Communist China had extended to Indonesia almost $1.5 billion in various forms of aid by the end of 1963. But a series of Alice-in-Wonderland snafus will probably add another $500 million to the cost of this aid. For example, the cost of a 200-bed hospital in Jakarta was originally set at $1 million; Indonesia's 100 per cent inflation made the bill $2 million. A 325-mile Russian-financed road through the Borneo jungle had to be "restudied" in the fall of 1963 to find ways of cutting the cost by 20 per cent because of rising prices. Meanwhile, Russian machinery shipped to Borneo more than a year earlier stood idle and rusting. Similarly, $6.5 million worth of equipment for a Soviet steel mill was still waiting for the start of that project, which was to have processed the iron ore carried over the road nobody had got around to building. Nearly $1 million worth of Hungarian buses were in mothballs because of the lack of spare parts.

Such Russian failures have been repeated elsewhere throughout the world. Even aid commitments to the Soviets' disaffected Red Chinese ally brought recriminations. The Chinese charged that Russian demands for payments on loans and credits contributed to food shortages and that poor Russian machinery hurt rather than helped Chinese industry. With few exceptions Russian rubles failed even to buy respectability for home-grown Communists around the world. In most countries they were either suppressed or outlawed. This was true even in those emerging and/or unstable countries where hopes might have seemed brightest for a quick political return on the rubles invested. Investments of $6 million in Tunisia, a like amount in Algeria, $12 million in Morocco, $1 billion in India, $317 million in Iraq and $715 million in the United Arab Republic bought, among other things, cracked heads for the local Communists.

If South Vietnam bit the American hand, some beneficiaries of Soviet aid gnawed the Russian arm right up to the elbow. India, studiously neutral in her East-West dealings, showed considerably less forbearance for Communists at home, a tendency which *Pravda* noted with "increasing alarm." Rather than throw in with the mad-dog policy of her own Red Chinese comrades, however, Russia was forced by the pressures of nuclear world politics to continue her aid commitments, taking India's side against her menacing Red neighbor to the north.

The United Arab Republic's Gamal Abdel Nasser proved another sticky ingrate. Just what Russian aid had bought beyond his rather consistent vote in the United Nations was not altogether clear. His behavior in his own back yard lent little support to the Soviet theory about how foreign aid was supposed to work. First there was to be a "national bourgeois" revolution, an ephemeral thing. Then the aid commitments were to pay off with a Communist take-over.

Nasser, however, persisted in his "national bourgeois" habit of imprisoning troublesome local Communists and, when the occasion seemed to call for it, executing them. Khrushchev was known to have protested about this personally to U.A.R. visitors. It just did not seem a fitting thing for Nasser to be doing in light of all the arms and aid Russia had provided.

And don't forget the Aswan Dam. This was the Soviets' big "impact" project in Egypt. They moved in on it when the United States, after a spat with Nasser, declined to take it on. It was to be a high dam on the Upper Nile that would provide water to irrigate some 2,000,000 arid acres. It was begun in 1960, but construction lagged from the start. Western-trained Egyptian engineers found the Russian engineers to be inferior, their equipment shoddy, their supply lines leaky and the Russians themselves an uncongenial crew. Meanwhile, Nasser's propaganda mills played down Russia's investment in the dam. By 1963 Russian aid to the project amounted to $325 million, repayable at 2 per cent interest after the dam was finished. As far as Nasser and his government were concerned, this was their dam, which, incidentally, the Russians were privileged to help build.

Nasser's commitment to the Soviet bloc, it seems clear, was a matter of economic exigency rather than ideological identity. He paid for it heavily in terms of inferior Communist goods bought at fancy prices and by being unable even to buy equipment that would have been readily available in the West. India also had learned to look for costly gimmicks in Soviet aid offers, such as low-cost equipment that could be kept running only by purchase of high-cost spare parts.

So had just about every other country Russia had set out to "help."

By the spring of 1963 our Agency for International Development estimated that total annual economic aid from the Sino-Soviet bloc to nations outside the Iron Curtain had dropped by half to some $450 million in the preceding year. Russia had apparently shifted its emphasis from new commitments to the underdeveloped nations to trying to deliver on commitments already made. Of 480 projects to which the Soviets had committed themselves since the mid-1950s, only 120 had been completed.

Obviously concerned about the scope and cost of the commitment, Mother Russia set out to share the burden with her captive chicks. Poland, Czechoslovakia, Romania, Bulgaria and Hungary were included in a new agency designed to regulate the flow of Communist-bloc arms and economic aid to underdeveloped countries. Russia had used Czechoslovakia and other satellites primarily to fill arms commitments. Now, however, the captives were apparently to assume a greater share of the financial burden of proving to a skeptical world that "Communism is good for you." Russia was not abandoning the aid race, in which she was lagging, but seemingly she was trying to cut her own economic losses.

And, along with her Red satellite colleagues, she was becoming increasingly impatient with apparent waste of her aid offerings. Early in October of 1963 after a hurricane tore up Cuba, Soviet-bloc representatives, meeting in Prague with a three-man Cuban commission, quickly came through with a promise of some $3.5 million in disaster relief. But they turned down a requested $500 million loan, with bitter complaints about Cuba's grossly mismanaged economy.

The Hungarian representative aimed a swift kick at the seat of Cuba's pants: "The whole of Cuba is full of militia who have nothing to guard, nothing to defend and nothing else to do except eat and take their salaries. But there is nobody to sweep the streets. Cuba, which should have been the example for the Western hemisphere of how socialism works, has become the prototype of how a rich country can be mismanaged by a few ignorant hotheads. . . ." The Soviet delegate commented, "We don't earn our export dollars to drop them into the Havana sewers." The Reds, in short, had much less wealth to throw around than we had—and it pained them proportionately more to see it squandered.

Such statements typified Russia's heavy-handed conduct of her aid program. Although her aid was offered on tighter terms than ours, it was usually initiated with greater fanfare. The recipient country was led to expect more than Russia either could or intended to deliver. Immediate political propaganda rather than long-term economic development was usually the goal. Thus, when we rejected a plea from Afghanistan to pave the streets of the capital city of Kabul as being outside the scope of our program, Russia moved in and did the job, pointing with pride all the while.

Professor Morgenthau would fault us for this, contending that we had "mistaken prestige aid" for economic aid and thereby had missed a chance to buy some political advantage practically for peanuts. Without rejecting Professor Morgenthau's argument out of hand, one might have some serious reservations about it. One is that such prestige as might accrue from such a project is likely to stick to the local politician who begged it. He would be more likely to invite local attention to "what I got for you" than "what they did for you," at least as long as the road was in good repair. Thereafter he would be not unlikely to complain about the poor engineering job that the donor had done. This, you will recall, was our experience with the "prestige" Cambodian highway. The only effective way for the donor to restore his own prestige in these circumstances is to return to patch the potholes, a not altogether seemly pastime for a great power.

Another reservation is that "prestige" aid is more easily administered by a dictatorship than a democracy. Grumbling of autoless Muscovite officials was reported when hard-to-get Russian cars were shipped to little Guinea. But dictatorships can with comparative impunity administer any kind of aid anywhere any time they want to. The peasant who is paying for it probably does not know about it and would not dare grouse much about it if he did. Not so the American taxpayer. He not only knows about such expenditures but sounds off about them. If he sounds off loud enough he is heard in Congress, and knives are sharpened for the next foreign aid budget. And if the knives cut too deeply the program might be imperiled.

One "prestige" gift in 1960, for instance, probably did as much to haunt our aid program and arm its critics as any offering before or since. This was the expenditure of $3.1 million to refit one of our World War II seaplane tenders for use by the Ethiopian Navy. The ship was air-conditioned and included a fancy suite for Emperor Haile Selassie. Outraged aid opponents immediately tagged it "the Emperor's yacht." Aid officials sought to justify the expense on grounds that the ship was to be used as both a training vessel and flagship of the Ethiopian Navy. As Commander in Chief, the Emperor would, of course, sometimes be aboard. That Ethiopia even had a Navy caught many Americans by surprise. That its flagship was a vintage seaplane tender on loan from the United States seemed to throw into some doubt the Ethiopian Navy's ability to help in time of mutual peril. This was, in fact, "prestige" aid, and the story of the Emperor's yacht plowed once again through the storied waves of Congressional debate about whether or not to cut the fiscal 1964 foreign aid bill.

But the case of the Emperor's yacht was a mere dinghy on the vast sea of so-called rivalry between the United States and the Soviet Union in the foreign aid field. What was significant was that time after time the United States had "reacted" to the Soviet bluff rather than proceed with its foreign aid program on the rational grounds of genuine need abroad and the national self-interest. It is now a footnote of history that as long ago as 1955–56 an attempt by Congress to begin the liquidation of foreign aid was foiled by this same fear of "What will the Russians do?" In retrospect, most people will probably agree that it was a good thing this radical move was derailed, but that does not make Uncle Sam's reaction at the time any less silly.

In late 1954 and early 1955, there was growing sentiment that the time had come to reduce our foreign aid program substantially. President Eisenhower was saying things like: "The United States cannot be an Atlas; it cannot, by its financial sacrifices, carry all other nations of the world on its own shoulders, and we should stop giveaway programs." Secretary of the Treasury George Humphrey, Under Secretary of State Herbert Hoover, Jr., and Budget Director Rowland R. Hughes were agitating for a big cutback.

Congress took the administration at its word. It ordered the Foreign Operations Agency liquidated and, shortly before its adjournment in July, 1955, set up a new organization, the International Cooperation Administration (ICA), to administer economic aid under the Department of State. Military aid was assigned to the Department of Defense.

Subsequently, President Eisenhower summoned his foreign aid advisers to Gettysburg during the first week of December, 1955, to set a figure for fiscal 1957. Shortly, the news was leaked that it had been decided to ask only $2.7 billion, the same as voted the previous year. Obviously, the conservatives had won out; Nelson A. Rockefeller resigned from the President's advisory staff in protest against the cut, and the ECA director, John Hollister, a former law partner of the late Senator Robert A. Taft, was in great good spirits.

But less than a week after letting it be known that the White House would go along with Congress in cutting back foreign aid, Secretary of State John Foster Dulles announced a change in signals. The administration, he said, would ask, not a mere $2.7 billion, but a whopping $4.9 billion for foreign aid. Additionally, it would ask Congress to approve a ten-year commitment of $100 million annually so that projects could be tackled on a long-range basis.

Whether this was good or not, the fact is that the change of mind was another reaction to Russian politicians. Administration sources admitted that the experts had decided more money would have to be requested because they were worried about recent Soviet gestures toward the so-called neutralist nations. Especially, they were concerned about the triumphal tour of Nikita Khrushchev and the then Soviet premier, Nicolai A. Bulganin, through India, Burma and Afghanistan. The Russians, it was noted, had been talking big. They had promised India a $30 million steel mill, ore-mining machinery and other heavy-industry goods. Russia and her satellites had been pledged to buy half of the Burmese rice crop in return for Burmese payment for Soviet help in expanding its agriculture and industry. Afghanistan was offered a $100 million credit for the purchase of machinery from the Soviet Union.

President Eisenhower admitted we were running scared in his message to Congress: "With the Soviet leaders openly proclaiming their world aim, it would be folly for us and our friends to relax our collective efforts toward stability and security." Secretary Dulles told the Senate Foreign Relations Committee, "The President regards the assistance program as vitally important to our people . . . an indispensable part of our national effort . . . necessary for the security of the United States." But when Dulles was asked for a bill of particulars which would tell the taxpayers what the foreign aid program had accomplished, he refused to do so. "We don't think it would be profitable to do this," he said. "Many of the projects are joint efforts with other countries [and] we don't want to give the impression we are taking too much credit."

The House promptly slashed a little over $1.1 billion from the administration request and vetoed the proposal for a $100 million blank check per year for ten years. But the White House applied pressure to the Senate, always more responsive to the wishes of the executive branch, and the Senate voted $4.2 billion. This was whittled down in a joint House-Senate conference, and the foreign aid bill, as finally passed, gave the administration $3.7 billion plus—a billion dollars more than it originally had said was needed.

Once again the Kremlin had called the tune.

12 *Quo Vadis?*

At the outset the authors confessed themselves some-what reluctant dragons. If a wisely spent foreign aid dollar can help keep the Cold War from heating up, we are for its expenditure. If there is a rational, even though financially risky, plan to help underdeveloped countries find and follow the path toward economic stability and political self-determination, we are for that, too. But like our tax-paying fellows we object strenuously to boneheaded waste by bureaucrats who seek to justify their own substantial salaries by indiscriminately committing our aid dollars to ill-planned enterprises abroad.

In this we are obviously not alone. The temper of the nation was reflected when the 88th Congress put the paring knife to foreign aid. There was a large and growing conviction that the costs of our program had proved disproportionate to its results. This raises the question of whether popular disgruntlement will one day soon spell an end to the program.

The answer would seem to be "no" for a number of reasons. There are indications that our program has been substantially refined by the fire of popular outrage at past evidence of waste and frippery; that in both concept and administra-

182

tion it has been tightened up; and that its administrators have finally come to the long-overdue conclusion that if the program is to survive they had best be frank with the man who pays the bills, the taxpayer.

There was, in fact, some irony in the timing of the crescendo of public dissatisfaction. It came at a time when our program was better organized and comparatively less costly than it ever had been. Since the Marshall Plan, our program had had a succession of ten administrators, who averaged only some sixteen months in office. They included such disparate types as the Marshall Plan's supersalesman Paul Hoffman; John B. Hollister, who took on the job despite his original disbelief in foreign aid; and Harold Stassen, former political wonder boy who operated out of his hat. The agency's name changed almost as often as its administrators. Aid philosophies shifted. Morale was low; personnel turnover high.

The eleventh administrator was David E. Bell. He was a specialist in long-range program planning. He had a master's degree from Harvard in economics and had both lectured there and served as chief administrative officer of Harvard's Graduate School of Public Administration. He had also worked variously on President Truman's White House staff and had done a couple of turns within the Budget Bureau. He was director of the Budget Bureau when President Kennedy tapped him for the tough and largely thankless job of heading up the Agency for International Development.

The combination of planner Bell and the concept of AID as a super-agency to coordinate our various economic assistance efforts boded well for the program. Only time would tell whether this apparently happy alliance could do a more effective and economically justifiable job than predecessor agencies had done. But the omens were good.

When foreign aid was attacked, Bell and his co-workers

frequently replied with some justification that the antagonists were talking about programs that used to be, rather than the one that was. The new AID approach put much more emphasis on our own self-interest. Thus:

Sixty per cent of our aid in fiscal 1964 would be in loans, a number of them contingent upon the recipient country's showing a willingness to help itself at the same time. This contrasted to Marshall Plan days when our aid was 90 per cent grants.

Some 80 per cent of our economic assistance would be tied to the purchase of goods within the United States. This would help our balance of payments, bolster the domestic economy, and create a foreign market for our goods that would, at least theoretically, survive the aid program itself.

The new line seemed to take into closer account the natural limitations of the program, and tailor the kind of aid to the country to which it was offered. Said Bell, "Fundamentally, AID's purpose is national security. By national security, we also mean a world of independent nations capable of making economic and social progress through free institutions. Economically, we're not aiming for standards of living; we're aiming for internal dynamics, self-sustaining growth. In each case we've tried to set down and assess what the needs and interests of the United States are there, where the country and its government are going, what they are doing in the way of self-help, what other advanced nations are or should be doing there. We have tried to apply a cold and realistic eye, and look several years ahead."

A corollary of our demand that donees be willing to help themselves was a readiness to withhold funds if they did not. AID withheld some $100 million for just such cause during fiscal 1963 and requested that much less in the new budget, Bell reported. There was also a move toward greater selectivity in programing aid funds. Of the $2.2 billion committed by AID in fiscal 1963, four-fifths went to only twenty countries, where the United States interests were deemed the most urgent. In some areas, like most of Africa, where France and the United Kingdom still had their own history of aid, our commitments were deliberately limited.

There was also a healthy trend toward outspoken United States insistence that other countries pick up a larger share of the aid burden that for years we carried alone. Western Europe, Japan and Canada were putting up some 40 per cent of the aid that went to underdeveloped countries. We were putting up 60 per cent. Furthermore, our aid was in long-term, low-interest-rate loans—an average of 2.6 per cent over 30 years—while the average for the other countries was 5 per cent for 19 years.

The major push by the United States was toward getting our allies to soften their interest rates and extend maturity dates on their loans. The 60-to-40 ratio of actual dollar aid conformed closely to the ratio of the United States gross national product to the gross national product of all the other countries. In fact, Bell contended, some few countries were putting a larger share of their gross national product into foreign aid than we were.

In April of 1963 the Development Assistance Committee, composed of representatives from the United States, Western Europe, Japan and Canada, agreed that loan terms should take into account the balance-of-payments prospects of the recipient country and that some lending countries should therefore soften their loan terms. By September of 1963 Bell was able to report:

"There had been some considerable softening by some countries prior to this agreement, and there has been some additional change since. The United Kingdom, for example, has cut the effective rate of interest on aid loans nearly in half. The Germans have begun to make much longer term loans, including as much as seven-year grace periods. Nevertheless, the United States government believes that there is a considerable distance still to go before there will be what we would consider an equitable sharing of foreign-aid costs among the advanced countries."

Indeed, Europe even had some way to go in sharing the cost of her own defense. Although we were "phasing out" our military aid to the Continent, as late as 1962 we were still pouring in more than $370 million, Italy being the largest recipient with $70.7 million. This was in addition to our own troops stationed there. In 1951 the United States had agreed to supply the equivalent of six infantry divisions as an emergency reinforcement for NATO while Europe was getting back on her feet. Twelve years later they were still there. By October of 1963 former President Eisenhower was publicly voicing his belief that it was high time to bring some of the troops home.

"I believe the time has now come when we should start withdrawing some troops," General Eisenhower said in a *Saturday Evening Post* article. "I believe the United States has the right and the duty of insisting that her NATO partners assume more of the burden of defending Western Europe." Withdrawal of United States troops would both ease the drain on American dollars and encourage West European countries to develop their own military strength, he argued.

Insistence that our European friends take on a greater share of mutual defense costs was amply justified by the postwar prosperity that our $30 billion in Marshall Plan gifts had brought to the Continent. For Europe was not only rich, but was using the protectionist policies of her Common Market to wax richer, in part at our expense.

Although we had urged the creation of an economically and politically unified Europe, it was our goal that she should become a strong and equal partner in an Atlantic Community. This close partnership between a revived Europe and the United States would weld the richest, most industrialized and powerful nations of the world into an ever-expanding community to which the underdeveloped and uncommitted nations would be naturally attracted.

By late 1963 this goal had been realized only in part, due largely to the obstructionism of French President Charles de Gaulle, who had visions of France's dominating Europe and Europe's occupying an increasingly independent role in world affairs. He insisted that France have her own nuclear capability, independent of the United States and Britain, whom he called "the Anglo-Saxons," and blackballed Britain's entry into the Common Market. Meanwhile, the high tariff policies of the Common Market were causing increasing concern to the United States.

In reaction to the Market's economic challenge, President Kennedy asked for and the Congress passed the Trade Expansion Act of 1962 to lower our own tariffs in return for like favors from the six-nation European bloc. Some economic thinkers took the position that our Marshall Plan aid should have been administered with the possibility of such an economic dilemma in view. We should have conditioned our gifts on pledges against Europe's return to a policy of protectionism, the argument went. Our Marshall Plan goal had been essentially political—to prevent Communist exploitation of the economic chaos that prevailed after the war, particularly in France and Italy. It was realized admirably. Some economists argued, however, that in gearing our economic aid to political purposes without having assured ourselves of its long-range economic results we had limited its effectiveness and sown the seeds of our own crop of future problems.

At the time our Marshall Plan was born we enjoyed nu-

clear supremacy, political pre-eminence and the only industrial complex among the major nations that had emerged
unscathed from the war. We could have written our own
ticket. To the extent that we did have an economic goal in
administering Marshall Plan aid, however, it was largely
limited to creating in a revived Europe a market with sufficient dollar capacity to buy our exports. Long unaccustomed
to dealing with economies of breadth or vigor comparable
to our own, we were not at that time prepared to examine
seriously the possibility that our aid would change this picture. Belatedly, we realized that our aid money had replaced
demolished industrial plants with newer and more efficient
ones than many of our own. This factor, combined with
Europe's long history of managerial talent, skilled labor and
lower wage rates, posed new and more difficult trade chal-
lenges for us. The fantastic economic growth and cohesion
of the European economic complex had far exceeded the
most sanguine estimates when our Marshall Plan was
launched. A similar growth pattern, due in large part to our
postwar aid, was apparent in Japan.

Thus it is reasonable to assume that these industrial nations, at our firm insistence, will over the years enlarge their
aid participation in common cause with us. To the extent
that they do, our own aid efforts will be further committed,
although, we would hope, on a somewhat smaller scale. Not
the least likely reason for our continued participation would
be a foreign aid record that, despite the waste, the boondoggles and the boners, added up to something fairly im-
pressive over the years. As of late 1963, AID could report
that of forty-one countries that since 1945 had received
$350 million or more in aid, thirty-three had achieved growth
rates of at least 1.5 per cent per capita for at least five years.

Director Bell was also reporting "definite plans" to end our
economic help to such countries as Israel, Nationalist China,

Mexico, Venezuela and Greece within two to five years, although military aid would continue in such strategically vital countries as Greece and Formosa. Such successes, rich in some areas, meager in others, would count for something even if our basic aim were pure do-goodism.

The fact is, of course, that this is not the aim. Bell, President Kennedy and others were coming around to the realization that if they were to preserve the program they would have to start saying so rather bluntly. Thus, on August 30, 1963, a Washington report from the Scripps-Howard Newspapers' foreign affairs writer, Walter Friedenberg, led off with this significant observation:

For the first time, Foreign Aid Director David E. Bell has referred publicly to the one, great unmentionable motive of American aid programs: To gain desired political ends. Normally, United States officials from the President down say our aid is aimed at "assisting other countries to maintain their national independence and become economically self-supporting." That's true, but it's so blandly stated that it tells only half the story. Foreign aid, our top policy makers know, is international politics. But they're not supposed to say so aloud. The rationale for the hush-up: What would be gained here by injecting more realism into the annual debate on foreign aid would be lost through the resentment stirred up in the recipient countries.

There was a growing realization, however, that the sensibilities of the donees would have to be given secondary consideration. A foreign nation would have to be mortally offended to turn down our multimillion-dollar gifts, and experience with our aid program had not established that foreign sensibilities were very often that acute. The alternative was more dangerous. It was that the American taxpayer would tire of watching his dollars go abroad to regimes characterized neither by democracy as he understood it nor by apparent zeal in support of United States positions.

After nearly two decades of running an aid program, some plain talk about it was long overdue. It was not a cure-all. It would not by itself make everybody like us or agree with us all the time. It was only one tool of diplomacy. It was sometimes abused and cost us more than it should. To the extent that it was stupidly administered—too much spent in the wrong place at the wrong time for an unattainable end—much of it was wasted. It was a gamble that did not always pay off. But on balance it was a valuable tool with which to try to shape world affairs, present and future, to our liking. It was not cheap—but it was cheaper than blood.

That our aid effort should be based on political self-interest does no discredit to the humanitarian impulse that motivates some of our programs. The happiest example of an essentially humanitarian program is the Peace Corps, established September 22, 1961, to help underdeveloped countries meet their needs for trained manpower and promote international understanding. After two years of operation the Corps had demonstrated that people-to-people service, sometimes under conditions of extreme hardship, is the best kind of international politics.

For instance, "Death to the Yankees" signs greeted Peace Corps volunteers on their arrival in Peru. But in the Andes Mountain city of Arequipa volunteer American construction tradesmen, social workers and sanitation workers pitched in to help build decent housing and improve living conditions in the city's slums. They taught the natives carpentry, masonry and electrical skills, and at the University of Arequipa they taught chemistry and English. By 1963 their work was so universally recognized that more than 2,000 Peruvians were on hand to watch President Fernando Belaunde present the Peace Corps volunteers of Arequipa with the Silver Medal for public service, awarded annually on the anniversary of the city's founding.

Their reception in Asia was similar. On August 31, 1963, some 1,200 volunteers serving in eleven Asian countries received the Ramón Magsaysay Award for International Understanding, often called the "Nobel Prize of Asia." They were the first group of Americans ever to receive the award, which was established in 1958 to honor the late President of the Philippines.

The citation said of the volunteers: "The problem of achieving peace amidst the tensions and dangers of a nuclear age occupies the mind of much of the human race, yet few within it discover a useful way to contribute. In reaffirming the essential community of interest of all ordinary people, regardless of creed or nationality, the Peace Corps volunteers belong to that small but growing fraternity who by their individual efforts do make a difference."

In Africa, even left-leaning, West-baiting Kwame Nkrumah feted volunteers at the end of their two-year stint in Ghana. By the end of its second year, the Corps had 6,633 volunteers serving, or in training to serve, in forty-nine countries—2,513 in Latin America, 2,195 in Africa, 1,172 in the Far East, and 753 in the Near East and South Asia.

They were a young and diverse group of more or less average Americans with skills that might be taken for granted at home, but which meant the difference between continued stagnation and a step up in underdeveloped areas of the world. Although there was a smattering of oldsters in the Corps, the average age was twenty-five years and four months. They were doctors and specialists in pig raising; teachers and truck farmers; tractor drivers and experts in egg production; veterinarians and malaria control experts; architects and soil analysts.

The Peace Corps had proved a useful arm of the aid effort for several reasons, not the least of which was that it was universally understood. The American taxpayer, remembering his own rural traditions of community barn-raisings, readily understood this kind of people-to-people, shoulder-to-shoulder work. The host countries also understood. Originally planned as a corps of 10,000, it had by its second birthday requests from host countries for twice that number.

America could take pride, also, in the Corps' toughness. During the first nineteen months of its activities abroad, only seventeen volunteers out of a total of 4,126 assigned to foreign countries had to be evacuated to the United States because of emotional disorders. And only ten others were returned home because of serious organic illnesses. Six volunteers died, four in plane crashes, one in an auto accident and one of amoebiasis, a severe type of dysentery. Corps doctors reported that the volunteers suffered mostly from gastroenteritis (inflammation of the stomach and intestines) because they insisted on sacrificing personal hygiene in order to gain native "grass-roots" acceptance.

The Corps was also a comparatively inexpensive operation. It cost about $9,000 a year to select, train, transport and maintain abroad one volunteer, or, according to the Corps, about what it cost private missionary groups. Each country in which the volunteers served also provided some form of goods or services, based on the country's economic ability to do so. By the end of the second year these contributions had come to some $3.3 million.

The Corps provided a further saving in that its presence in a developing country could establish our interest more effectively and at less cost. Too often we had been bamboozled into undertaking costly "impact" projects that imposed the trappings of the twentieth century on an economically and politically primitive society. We had built roads that natives could not keep up. We had sent tractors where a hoe was needed. The Peace Corps was going in with a hoe. Whether it could resist the fatal urge, common to so

many Federal agencies, to expand into a big new bureaucracy remained for time to tell. But by the end of its second
year, it had done a good deal to restore some public sympathy for the aid concept.

This is not to say that the Corps' fresh approach to foreign
aid "saved" the program, which, beneath the clouds of occa-
sional public outrage, rested on a rather broad base of popular support. It is often argued by the executive branch, in its
annual budget battles with Congress, that foreign aid is
handicapped by having no constituency. A Congressman is
not likely to lose votes at home by opposing foreign aid in
Washington, the argument goes. But it is not quite that clear-
cut. The program does have powerful advocates.

It is highly significant, for instance, that George Meany,
president of the AFL-CIO, was the sole dissenter among the
ten prominent citizens who served on the Clay committee,
which urged a scaling down of the volume of our aid. Labor
leader Meany recommended exactly the opposite. "AID
funds should be substantially increased and geared to the
increasing ability of AID personnel to implement a stepped-
up program," Meany said. ". . . Moscow, Peiping and various other centers of international Communism are arrogantly
attempting to intone the funeral oration of democracy in the
free world. More important, capitalizing on social and economic stagnation, they probe everywhere for areas of weakness where they can penetrate and dominate. We should
know this and we should accept the long-term costs of frus-
trating this enemy and reinforcing our own strength by supporting around us a community of resolute, prospering, free
world societies. The Agency for International Development
and our Military Assistance Programs, wisely administered,
are insurance against possible vast military expenditures and
sacrifices of American lives, so great as to overshadow the
cost of this insurance. I do not accept the view that we can-

not afford to pay the full cost of these essential programs, nor, I am confident, do the people of the United States."

At the other pole, the United States Chamber of Commerce was also supporting the program, although it applauded the Clay committee majority while doing so. The central point is, however, that top spokesmen for both labor and the business community were backing foreign aid, a fact that attests to the degree to which the program had woven itself into the American economy. Through years of creating markets for American goods abroad, and thus creating jobs at home, it had created a strong nationwide "constituency." With our aid effort increasingly tied to foreign purchase of United States goods, it seemed unlikely that this support would wane.

A corollary to the "jobs-and-markets" rationale for support of foreign aid was the contention that the program had got progressively "cheaper" over the years—although nobody was contending that the annual outlays were insubstantial. By mid-1963 Deputy AID Administrator Frank M. Coffin was telling the League of Women Voters (another staunch advocate of foreign aid), "The facts are that fifteen years ago we were spending over 2 per cent of our gross national product and 11.5 per cent of our budget on aid. Today aid accounts for less than seven-tenths of 1 per cent of our gross national product, less than 4 per cent of our total budget, and less than one-twelfth of our budget for defense and security. By this I do not mean to minimize the investment—but I do suggest that we can afford the money."

Anti-foreign aid arguments that foreign aid cuts were needed to ease the United States' balance-of-payments problem were met with the counterargument that a $1 billion aid cut would reduce our balance-of-payments deficit by only $200 million—while reducing our exports by $800 million. A further argument was that our balance-of-payments position was being improved by repayment of earlier loans, and would be further improved over the years as outstanding loans were repaid.

Some of the most vocal criticism of aid among those who know the program best—members of Congress—turns on discontent with individual policies rather than the concept of foreign aid. Thus, in considering the 1964 program, Senate Foreign Relations Committee Chairman J. William Fulbright of Arkansas sponsored an amendment authorizing the use of aid funds to provide birth control information to poor countries. The population explosion in some underdeveloped nations had "substantially or entirely negated the benefits of United States economic assistance."

Senator Albert Gore of Tennessee, another committeeman, would end all military assistance to Latin America. "I see no reason why we should be arming forces down there to overthrow elected governments," he said. The whole "liberal revolt" in the Senate really turned on individual programs and the administration of aid, rather than on the aid principle itself. Thus in reporting the authorization bill to the Senate, the Foreign Relations Committee urged an end of aid to "countries that can take care of themselves," reduced aid to Spain and Portugal, increased use of such multilateral agencies as the World Bank, and strong United States insistence that other wealthy nations pick up more of the aid burden.

Such was the temper of Congress on November 14, 1963, that President Kennedy was asked at his news conference what the United States would do "in the event that one of these years Congress, the arguments for foreign aid notwithstanding, surprises itself by voting the program out."

Kennedy conceded that in 1963 the program had come under the "worst attack that we've seen since the beginning of the Marshall Plan," but he defended its usefulness as a foreign policy tool. "I can't imagine anything more dangerous than to end this program," he said. ". . . I think it's a very dangerous, untidy world, but we're going to have to live with it and I think one of the ways to live with it is to permit us to function." President Kennedy was pleading with Congress not to tie his hands by slashing aid or unreasonably restricting its use.

Later that same day, Senator Morse, who spearheaded the forces of revolt, appeared in the Senate chamber with a two-foot-high stack of reports from the Comptroller General's office. Rasped Morse, "They are not pleasant reading, for I engage in no understatement when I say that any jury that read them could not bring back any other verdict than that these reports . . . show that hundreds and hundreds of millions of dollars of the American taxpayers' money have been wasted. . . .

"The administration does not like to hear anyone criticize the foreign aid program for waste. It is easy to say, as many apologists for the program have been heard to say, 'You cannot have a program involving billions of dollars that the foreign aid program involves without a considerable amount of waste.' But we do not have to have that kind of waste. We do not have to have waste to that degree."

Ironically, the gravest threat to the foreign aid program was itself. Although impartial public opinion polls showed Americans supported the principle, there was a danger that wasteful administration would one day bring about a complete collapse of public and Congressional support. Indeed, the program had in part been protected from self-destruction by those enemies who criticized it most cruelly. During one of his periodic workings-over of the program, Representative "Otto the Terrible" Passman told AID Administrator Bell:

"Mr. Administrator, a member of the Clay committee told me that, had it not been for this [appropriations] subcommittee, foreign aid would very likely have fallen of its own weight on account of the ridiculously high amounts requested. . . . He said that in his opinion had it not been for this subcommittee acting as a brake on spending there would probably be no foreign aid program now."

Passman wanted to know if Bell also had been so advised. Bell said he had not. Untroubled, Passman concluded, "It was, I thought, a fine compliment to the work of this subcommittee, which has so often been accused of 'wrecking' the program."

And so it was. Foreign aid can deal with its enemies, such as Otto Passman, and often come out the stronger for it. Its real danger lies in the glandular thinking of its free-spending friends, who believe because it is good it has no need to be businesslike. Helping other nations that need help is one of the pillars of America's foreign policy, but it cannot be approached with the casual air of a stroller tossing two bits to a street-corner beggar. This is an insult to the needy nations as well as a crime against the American taxpayer. It is time the administrators of the program took heed of President Johnson's call, in his first message to Congress, to gather together and "negotiate the national interest."

Appendix

CONGRESSIONA

TABLE I — *Total foreign aid, by regio*

Region and country	Grand total	Total military	ECONOMIC				
			Total economic	AID programs			
				AID total	Technical cooperation/ development grants	Development loans	Other AID
Total, all countries	103,916	32,284	71,632	35,967	1,990	4,356	29,62
Near East and south Asia	20,224	5,613	14,611	8,022	566	2,738	4,71
Afghanistan	237	3	235	152	53	3	9
Ceylon	88		88	26	10	6	
Cyprus	21		21	4	1	2	
Greece	3,516	1,682	1,834	1,082	14	85	98
India	4,718	60	4,658	1,890	159	1,388	34
Iran	1,422	633	789	592	72	138	38
Iraq	69	46	22	19	17		
Israel	962	5	957	464	11	146	30
Jordan	414	30	385	317	36	3	27
Lebanon	88	9	80	58	18	5	3
Nepal	53		53	31	18	(1)	
Pakistan	2,227	(2)	2,227	1,344	67	615	66
Saudi Arabia	46	(2)	46	27	2		2
Syrian Arab Republic	96	(1)	96	32	(1)	23	
Turkey	4,164	2,403	1,761	1,336	43	252	1,04
United Arab Republic (Egypt)	807		807	175	14	72	9
Yemen	27	(1)	27	17			1
Cento	28		28	28	2		2
Regional	1,240	743	497	427	26		40
Latin America	7,928	716	7,212	1,862	479	759	62
Argentina	773	48	726	155	8	127	2
Bolivia	334	8	326	225	35	34	5
Brazil	2,123	231	1,892	225	84	112	2
British Guiana	5		5	4	4		
British Honduras	3		3	1	1		(1)
Chile	840	76	764	260	30	94	3
Colombia	547	60	487	172	29	112	3
Costa Rica	105	1	104	36	14	20	
Cuba	52	11	42	3	3		
Dominican Republic	100	11	89	58	6	2	4
Ecuador	184	34	149	77	29	28	2
El Salvador	65	3	62	33	14	18	(1)
Guatemala	178	7	171	99	24	14	6
Haiti	106	6	100	62	13	5	4

Footnotes at end of table.

[In millions of 1946 dollars]

RECORD—SENATE

country and category, 1946 to 1963.

ASSISTANCE

		Other economic assistance							
		Food for peace—Public Law 480							
			Title I						
Total	Social progress trust fund	Total	Total sales agreements	Planned for country use	Title II	Title III	Title IV	Export-Import Bank long-term loans	Other economic programs
35,665	349	10,127	(8,337)	6,329	1,245	2,439	115	8,078	17,111
6,500	--------	4,822	(4,471)	3,786	440	596	--------	865	902
83	--------	43	(-----)	--------	42	1	--------	39	(1)
62	--------	62	(30)	22	9	30	--------	--------	(1)
17	--------	17	(1)	1	16	(1)	--------	--------	(1)
752	--------	194	(108)	74	4	116	--------	21	537
2,768	--------	2,225	(2,334)	2,036	9	180	--------	311	232
198	--------	95	(51)	37	45	13	--------	74	28
4	--------	3	(-----)	--------	--	3	--------	--------	1
493	--------	273	(244)	216	2	56	--------	220	(1)
68	--------	65	(-----)	--------	49	16	--------	2	1
22	--------	17	(-----)	--------	17	--------	--------	3	2
22	--------	21	(-----)	17	4	--------	--------	--------	1
882	--------	760	(715)	636	84	40	--------	51	71
19	--------	--------	(-----)	--------	--------	--------	--------	15	4
64	--------	59	(37)	29	28	2	--------	5	--------
425	--------	336	(430)	296	28	12	--------	75	13
632	--------	573	(520)	421	29	123	--------	48	11
9	--------	9	(-----)	--------	9	--------	--------	--------	--------
-------	--------	------	(-----)	--------	--------	--------	--------	-------	-------
70	--------	70	(-----)	--------	66	4	--------	--------	--------
5,350	349	957	(712)	561	77	264	55	3,452	592
571	35	18	(30)	18	--------	--------	--------	517	(1)
102	10	52	(25)	20	18	11	3	26	12
1,667	53	390	(385)	318	28	44	--------	1,177	48
1	--------	1	(-----)	--------	--------	1	--------	--------	--------
2	--------	2	(-----)	--------	(1)	1	--------	--------	(1)
504	24	132	(71)	56	--------	55	21	342	7
315	31	104	(69)	51	--------	47	7	172	7
68	4	3	(-----)	--------	2	1	--------	26	36
39	--------	1	(-----)	--------	--------	1	--------	38	1
31	6	13	(-----)	--------	--------	7	5	10	2
72	24	20	(12)	8	(1)	7	4	24	5
30	12	6	(-----)	--------	--------	4	2	10	2
73	11	7	(-----)	--------	3	4	--------	17	38
39	--------	11	(-----)	--------	4	7	--------	25	3

TABLE I— *Total foreign aid, by region*

Region and country	Grand total	Total military	ECONOMIC				
			Total economic	AID programs			
				AID total	Technical cooperation/ development grants	Development loans	Other AID
Latin America—Con.							
Honduras	61	5	56	38	18	9	10
Jamaica	22		22	9	3	5	1
Mexico	817	6	810	29	8	20	1
Nicaragua	79	5	73	25	13	12	(¹)
Panama	110	1	109	49	17	14	18
Paraguay	70	2	67	36	20	14	2
Peru	509	97	412	87	36	42	8
Surinam	4		4	3	3		
Trinidad and Tobago	24		24	14	3		11
Uruguay	111	30	81	19	4	15	(¹)
Venezuela	329	64	265	60	5	55	(¹)
Other West Indies	2		2				
ROCAP	11		11	8	6	2	
Regional	363	8	354	76	47	5	24
Far East	23,474	8,807	14,667	7,844	366	397	7,081
Burma	108		108	55	2		53
Cambodia	367	97	270	267	32		235
China, Republic of	4,524	2,399	2,125	1,391	25	176	1,191
Hong Kong	36		36				
Indochina, undistributed	1,535	710	826	826	2		824
Indonesia	881	76	805	280	96	12	172
Japan	3,824	1,040	2,784	22	11		11
Korea	5,674	2,044	3,630	2,298	47	81	2,170
Laos	328	(²)	328	326	8		318
Malaya	25		25	20		20	
Philippines	1,851	423	1,428	278	45	35	198
Thailand	869	508	361	316	53	34	229
Vietnam	1,896	(²)	1,896	1,720	38	40	1,642
Western Samoa	(¹)		(¹)	(¹)			(¹)
Regional	1,556	1,510	46	45	6		39
Africa	2,405	146	2,256	1,367	295	324	746
Algeria	·95		95	2	1		
Burundi	6		6	(¹)	(¹)		
Cameroon	17	(¹)	17	16	1	9	5
Central African Republic	1		1	1	1		(¹)
Chad	2		2	1	1		(¹)
Congo: Brazzaville	2		2	2	2		(¹)

Footnotes at end of table.

[In millions of 1946 dollars]

country and category, 1946 to 1963.

ASSISTANCE

Other economic assistance

Total	Social progress trust fund	Food for peace—Public Law 480						Export-Import Bank long-term loans	Other economic programs
		Total	Title I		Title II	Title III	Title IV		
			Total sales agreements	Planned for country use					
18	6	3	(------)	--------	(¹)	3	--------	3	6
13	--------	8	(------)	--------		8		5	(¹)
782	19	46	(25)	·18	1	27		617	100
48	8	2	(------)			2		13	25
60	10	7	(------)			7		19	23
31	3	15	(13)	10		5		10	3
325	26	62	(33)	23	20	17	2	223	14
1	--------	1	(------)			1			--------
10	--------	(¹)	(------)			(¹)		9	(¹)
62	10	38	(48)	36	(¹)	2	--------	10	4
204	53	13	(------)			2	11	135	3
2	--------	2	(------)		(¹)	2			
3	3	--------	(------)						
278	1	--------	(------)					25	252
6,823	--------	1,482	(1,181)	950	118	406	8	840	4,501
53	--------	48	(51)	46	--------	3			.5
2	--------	2	(------)		2	(¹)			
734	--------	198	(137)	107	12	70	8	33	502
36	--------	36	(------)		4	32			
			(------)						
525	--------	293	(325)	280	1	12		164	68
2,762	--------	170	(146)	106	37	27		393	2,199
1,331	--------	472	(361)	313	24	136			859
2	--------	2	(------)		1	1			
5	--------	4	(------)			4			1
1,150	--------	76	(36)	26		50		218	857
45	--------	4	(4)	4		1		32	8
176	--------	176	(80)	69	37	70			
1			(------)						1
889	--------	608	(119)	99	408	97	4	198	82
92	--------	92	(------)		70	22			
6	--------	6	(------)		4	2			
1	--------	(¹)	(------)			(¹)			1
(¹)	--------	(¹)	(------)			(¹)			
(¹)	--------	(¹)	(------)			(¹)			
(¹)	--------		(------)					(¹)	

TABLE I— *Total foreign aid, by region*

Region and country	Grand total	Total military	ECONOMIC				
				AID programs			
			Total economic	AID total	Technical cooperation/development grants	Development loans	Other AID
Africa—Con.							
Léopoldville	242	3	239	177	7	----------	170
Dahomey	7	(¹)	6	3	1	----------	2
Ethiopia	212	80	133	93	45	34	15
Gabon	2	----------	2	1	1	----------	(¹)
Ghana	159	(¹)	159	90	7	82	1
Guinea	29	----------	29	20	6	2	12
Ivory Coast	13	(¹)	12	7	3	2	2
Kenya	24	----------	24	13	7	2	4
Liberia	179	6	173	80	39	34	6
Libya	206	7	198	132	25	5	103
Malagasy Republic	2	----------	2	2	1	----------	1
Mali, Republic of	11	2	9	9	1	2	6
Mauritania	2	----------	2	2	(¹)	----------	----------
Morocco	427	(²)	427	261	5	23	234
Niger	5	(¹)	5	4	2	1	2
Nigeria	81	(¹)	81	64	40	16	8
Rhodesia and Nyasaland	38	----------	38	16	5	----------	10
Rwanda	1	----------	1	----------	----------	----------	----------
Senegal	14	3	11	9	5	----------	(¹)
Sierra Leone	7	----------	7	5	4	----------	(¹)
Somali Republic	38	----------	38	32	19	6	7
Sudan	76	----------	76	68	17	16	35
Tanganyika	30	----------	30	14	4	9	----------
Togo	7	----------	7	3	2	----------	----------
Tunisia	364	(²)	364	198	16	78	105
Uganda	12	----------	12	11	7	4	(¹)
Upper Volta	4	(¹)	4	3	1	----------	2
Zanzibar	(¹)	----------	(¹)	(¹)	(¹)	----------	----------
Other French communities and possessions	6	----------	6	6	1	----------	5
Other British territories	1	----------	1	(¹)	(¹)	----------	(¹)
Portuguese possessions	13	----------	13	(¹)	(¹)	----------	----------
Regional	68	46	22	22	17	----------	6
Europe	**45,361**	**16,073**	**29,288**	**15,238**	**90**	**137**	**15,012**
Austria	1,208	----------	1,208	726	3	----------	724
Belgium-Luxembourg	1,988	1,247	741	560	1	----------	559
Denmark	928	626	302	281	2	----------	279
France	9,445	4,263	5,182	3,190	6	----------	3,184

Footnotes at end of table.

[In millions of 1946 dollars]

ountry and category, 1946 to 1963.

ASSISTANCE

Total	Social progress trust fund	Other economic assistance						Export-Import Bank long-term loans	Other economic programs
		Food for peace—Public Law 480							
		Total	Title I		Title II	Title III	Title IV		
			Total sales agreements	Planned for country use					
62	-----	62	(43)	38	18	6	-----	-----	-----
3	-----	3	(-----)	-----	2	2	-----	-----	-----
40	-----	14	(1)	1	10	2	1	22	4
1	-----	([1])	(-----)	-----	-----	([1])	-----	-----	1
70	-----	4	(-----)	-----	1	3	-----	65	1
9	-----	9	(9)	7	2	-----	-----	-----	([1])
6	-----	([1])	(-----)	-----	-----	([1])	-----	5	1
11	-----	11	(-----)	-----	10	1	-----	-----	-----
93	-----	4	(-----)	-----	-----	1	3	79	10
66	-----	35	(-----)	-----	28	7	-----	-----	31
1	-----	1	(-----)	-----	([1])	1	-----	-----	-----
([1])	-----	([1])	(-----)	-----	([1])	([1])	-----	-----	1
66	-----	165	(22)	16	111	37	-----	-----	-----
([1])									([1])
17	-----	1	(-----)	-----	-----	1	-----	12	5
23	-----	([1])	(-----)	-----	-----	([1])	-----	-----	23
1	-----	1	(-----)	-----	1	([1])	-----	-----	1
2	-----	1	(-----)	-----	-----	1	-----	([1])	2
3	-----	1	(-----)	-----	-----	1	-----	-----	1
6	-----	5	(-----)	-----	5	([1])	-----	-----	-----
8	-----	8	(11)	8	([1])	([1])	-----	-----	1
16	-----	16	(-----)	-----	15	1	-----	-----	-----
4	-----	4	(-----)	-----	2	1	-----	([1])	1
167	-----	163	(34)	28	130	5	-----	2	1
1	-----	1	(-----)	-----	([1])	1	-----	-----	-----
1	-----	1	(-----)	-----	-----	1	-----	-----	-----
([1])	-----	([1])	(-----)	-----	-----	([1])	-----	-----	-----
-----	-----		(-----)	-----	-----		-----	-----	-----
-----	-----	1	(-----)	-----	-----	1	-----	-----	-----
12	-----		(-----)	-----	-----		-----	12	-----
([1])	-----		(-----)	-----	-----		-----	-----	([1])
14,050	-----	2,008	(1,895)	933	174	853	47	2,722	9,320
482	-----	82	(41)	26	28	27	-----	72	328
181	-----	([1])	(-----)	-----	-----	([1])	-----	148	32
21	-----	-----	-----	-----	-----	-----	-----	20	1
1,992	-----	20	(36)	8	-----	12	-----	1,263	709

TABLE I—*Total foreign aid, by region*

Region and country	Grand total	Total military	ECONOMIC				
			Total economic	AID programs			
				AID total	Technical cooperation/ development grants	Development loans	Other AID
Europe—Continued							
Germany (Federal Republic)	5,001	951	4,050	1,472	2		1,470
Berlin	132		132	119	1		118
Iceland	72		72	60	·1		59
Ireland	146		146	146	(¹)		146
Italy (including Trieste)	6,006	2,316	3,691	1,650	5		1,645
Netherlands	2,472	1,242	1,230	992	1	3	987
Norway	1,174	822	352	277	2		275
Poland	533		533	65	4		61
Portugal	498	337	161	51	1		50
Spain	1,742	540	1,202	579	6	17	556
Sweden	109		109	107	(¹)		107
United Kingdom	8,711	1,037	7,674	3,835	6		·3,892
Yugoslavia	2,510	693	1,816	576	12	117	448
Regional	2,684	1,998	686	551	36		515
Nonregional	4,525	927	3,598	1,634	194		1,440

¹ Less than $500,000.

[In millions of 1946 dollars]

country and category, 1946 to 1963.

ASSISTANCE

Total	Social progress trust fund	Other economic assistance						Export-Import Bank long-term loans	Other economic programs
		Food for peace—Public Law 480							
		Total	Title I		Title II	Title III	Title IV		
			Total sales agreements	Planned for country use					
2,578	--------	140	(1)	--------	3	137	--------	9	2,428
13	--------	--------	(------)	--------					13
12	--------	12	(15)	12	--------	--------	--------	(1)	(1)
2,040	--------	445	(144)	98	92	255	--------	425	1,171
238	--------	(1)	(1)	--------	--------	(1)	--------	202	36
75	--------	(1)	(------)	--------		(1)		50	25
468	--------	26	(474)	--------		26		40	402
110	--------	55	(7)	3	--------	38	13	55	--------
623	--------	427	(506)	263	4	160	--------	197	
2	--------	--------	(------)	--------					2
3,839	--------	(1)	(48)	--------	--------	(1)	--------	2	3,837
1,240	--------	799	(622)	522	47	197	34	105	336
136	-------	1	(------)	1	--------	--------		135	
1,964	--------	250	(------)	--------	26	223	--------	--------	1,714

2 Military data classified and included in regional totals.

CONGRESSIONAl

TABLE II—*Foreign aid, fisca*

Region and country	Grand total 100 countries and territories	Total military	ECONOMIC				
			Total economic	AID total	AID programs		
					Development grants/ program social progress	Development loans	Supporting assistance and other
Total, all countries............	7,026.7	1,849.9	5,176.8	2,395.8	343.6	1,287.8	764.2
Near East and south Asia...............	2,288.0	380.3	1,907.7	983.9	54.0	779.6	150.3
Afghanistan...........	19.2	1.2	18.0	17.7	15.1	2.6	....
Ceylon...............	8.4	....	8.4	.4	.4	....	....
Cyprus...............	4.1	....	4.1	2.9	.6	2.3	....
Greece...............	128.8	79.6	49.2	31.6	....	31.6	....
India...............	821.0	30.0	791.0	402.3	6.3	396.0	....
Iran...............	115.9	58.1	57.8	23.4	3.8	17.4	2.2
Iraq...............	1.0	.1	.9	.8	.8	....	....
Israel...............	78.9	.6	78.3	45.0	....	45.0	....
Jordan...............	63.6	4.3	59.3	43.0	7.0	....	36.0
Lebanon...............	.3	.2	.1	.1	.1	....	....
Nepal...............	4.6	....	4.6	3.9	3.9	....	....
Pakistan...............	372.5	(³)	372.5	185.0	7.9	176.8	.3
Saudi Arabia...........	....	(³)	....	....	....	....	....
Syrian Arab Republic...............	.4	(⁴)	.4	.2	.2	....	(⁴)
Turkey...............	317.2	135.7	181.5	131.1	4.7	71.4	-55.0
United Arab Republic (Egypt).....	198.7	....	198.7	48.6	2.3	36.3	10.0
Yemen...............	4.0	(⁴)	4.0	3.4	....	....	3.4
CENTO...............	.8	....	.8	.8	.5	....	.3
Regional...............	148.5	70.5	78.0	43.5	.4	....	43.1
Latin America...........	1,102.7	⁶ 74.8	1,027.9	548.9	109.0	342.8	97.1
Argentina...............	156.5	2.7	153.8	99.7	3.3	76.4	20.0
Bolivia...............	69.9	1.6	68.3	35.7	7.5	18.3	9.9
Brazil...............	172.3	16.9	155.4	86.9	24.0	37.4	25.5
British Guiana.......	1.4	....	1.4	1.4	1.3	....	....
British Honduras.....	.6	....	.6	.1	.1	....	....
Chile...............	99.2	10.2	89.0	41.3	6.3	35.0	(⁴)
Colombia...............	134.9	8.4	126.5	93.5	6.1	87.2	.2
Costa Rica............	15.5	.7	14.8	13.0	2.4	10.6	....
Dominican Republic..	51.7	2.1	49.6	29.4	3.4	2.1	23.9
Ecuador...............	39.2	2.8	36.4	18.2	4.9	6.3	7.0
El Salvador...........	23.1	.6	22.5	19.6	3.0	16.6	....
Guatemala............	15.4	2.0	13.4	3.4	2.7	.7	....
Haiti...............	6.2	.4	5.8	4.9	....	....	4.9

Footnotes at end of table.

[In millions of dollars]

RECORD—SENATE

year 1963 (preliminary report).

ASSISTANCE

Other economic assistance

| Total | Social progress trust fund | Food for peace—Public Law 480 | | | Title II | Title III | Title IV | Export-Import Bank long-term loans | Other economic programs |
| | | Total | Title I | | | | | | |
			Total sales agreements	Planned for country use					
2,781.0	124.8	1,771.3	(1,268.2)	1,074.2	314.6	314.1	68.4	571.7	313.2
923.8	--------	854.4	(766.6)	682.0	111.5	60.9	--------	64.5	¹4.9
.3	--------	.1	(------)	--------	--------	.1	--------	--------	.2
8.0	--------	7.8	(4.7)	3.5	--------	4.3	--------	--------	.2
1.2	--------	1.1	²(1.1)	.9	--------	.2	--------	--------	.1
17.6	--------	14.6	(11.2)	6.5	--------	8.1	--------	3.0	--------
388.7	--------	347.5	²(373.3)	333.9	--------	13.6	--------	40.3	.9
34.4	--------	34.2	(7.7)	5.8	25.0	3.4	--------	--------	.2
.1	--------	.1	(------)	--------	--------	.1	--------	--------	--------
33.3	--------	22.1	²(23.2)	19.8	1.5	.8	--------	11.2	--------
16.3	--------	16.3	(------)	--------	14.4	1.9	--------	--------	--------
.7	--------	.2	(------)	--------	.2	--------	--------	--------	.5
187.5	--------	185.4	²(155.4)	146.1	35.5	3.8	--------	--------	2.1
.2	--------	.2	(------)	--------	--------	.2	--------	--------	--------
50.4	--------	49.8	²(55.9)	45.0	--------	4.8	--------	--------	.6
150.1	--------	140.1	²(134.1)	120.5	--------	19.6	--------	10.0	--------
.6	--------	.6	(------)	--------	.6	--------	--------	--------	--------
34.5	--------	34.5	(------)	--------	34.4	.1	--------	--------	--------
479.0	124.8	185.4	(63.6)	51.5	18.8	75.6	39.6	91.2	⁵77.6
54.1	30.0	--------	(------)	--------	--------	--------	--------	³24.1	--------
32.6	10.5	21.4	(16.9)	14.3	.4	3.7	3.0	--------	.7
68.5	5.8	61.6	(43.4)	34.7	11.3	15.6	--------	--------	1.1
.1	--------	.1	--------	--------	--------	.1	--------	--------	--------
.5	--------	.3	(------)	--------	--------	.3	--------	--------	.2
47.7	4.9	26.5	(------)	--------	--------	5.5	21.0	15.5	.8
33.0	8.5	18.3	(------)	--------	--------	11.5	6.8	3.4	2.8
1.8	--------	1.6	(------)	--------	1.5	.1	--------	--------	.2
20.2	6.5	12.5	(------)	--------	1.2	6.3	5.0	--------	1.2
18.2	9.9	6.1	(------)	--------	--------	2.3	3.8	1.3	.9
2.9	--------	2.6	(------)	--------	--------	2.6	--------	--------	.3
10.0	7.8	1.0	(------)	--------	--------	1.0	--------	--------	1.2
.9	--------	.9	(------)	--------	--------	.9	--------	--------	--------

TABLE II—*Foreign aid, fisca*

Region and country	Grand total 100 countries and territories	Total military	ECONOMIC				
			. Total economic	AID programs			
				AID total	Development grants/ program social progress	Development loans	Supporting assistance and other
Latin America—Con.							
Honduras	14.4	1.1	13.3	7.3	3.2	1.6	2.4
Jamaica	13.0	----	13.0	5.8	.8	5.0	
Mexico	50.9	.1.2	49.7	.4	.4		
Nicaragua	9.0	1.5	7.5	3.5	2.5	1.0	
Panama	10.0	.8	9.2	8.2	2.2	6.0	
Paraguay	10.2	.9	9.3	3.0	3.0		
Peru	31.0	6.7	24.3	3.0	3.0		
Surinam	.4	----	.4	.3	.3		
Trinidad and Tobago	4.1	----	4.1	3.9	.8		. 3.1
Uruguay	24.6	2.5	22.1	7.9	1.9	6.0	
Venezuela	56.8	10.4	46.4	33.1	3.0	30.0	.1
Other West Indies	.4	----	.4				
ROCAP	11.1	----	11.1	8.2	5.7	2.5	
Regional	80.4	1.2	79.2	17.2	17.0		
Far East	1,723.3	785.0	938.3	428.7	53.3	67.1	308.2
Burma	15.2	----	15.2	6.7	1.0		5.7
Cambodia	29.2	10.4	18.8	18.8	7.8		11.0
China, Republic of	212.6	132.3	80.3	38.6	2.1	36.5	
Hong Kong	5.6	----	5.6				
Indonesia	140.9	17.6	123.3	36.7	14.8		21.9
Japan	172.9	49.1	123.8				
Korea	403.7	199.4	204.3	. 126.2	5.6	30.6	90.0
Laos	36.8	(³)	36.8	36.3			36.3
Malaya	2.2	----	2.2				
Philippines	117.7	23.9	93.8	2.9	2.9		
Thailand	94.2	71.6	22.6	16.2	6.4		9.9
Vietnam	208.1	(³)	208.1	143.7	10.5		133.2
Regional	284.0	⁸ 280.8	3.2	2.5	2.2		.2
Africa	553.9	27.4	526.5	261.6	79.8	98.38	3.4
Algeria	79.6	----	79.6	1.8	1.1		.7
Burundi	1.5	----	1.5	(⁴)	(⁴)		
Cameroon	1.5	(⁴)	1.5	1.0	1.0		
Central African Republic	.7	----	.7	.7	.7		
Chad	1.1	----	1.1	1.0	1.0		
Congo:							
Brazzaville	.7	----	.7	.5	.5		
Léopoldville	79.8	.2	79.6	42.4	3.0		39.4
Dahomey	1.0	(⁴)	1.0	.7	.7		
Ethiopia	24.2	9.0	15.2	10.0	.0	4.0	

Footnotes at end of table.

[In millions of dollars]

year 1963 (preliminary report).

ASSISTANCE

Total	Social progress trust fund	Food for peace—Public Law 480						Export-Import Bank long-term loans	Other economic programs
		Total	Title I		Title II	Title III	Title IV		
			Total sales agreements	Planned for country use					
6.0	5.6	.3	(------)	------	------	.3	------	------	.1
7.2	------	2.0	(------)	------	------	2.0	------	5.0	.2
49.3	8.0	15.5	(------)	------	1.1	14.4	------	25.8	------
4.0	.2	1.4	(------)	------	------	1.4	------	------	2.4
1.0	------	.7	(------)	------	------	.7	------	------	.3
6.3	2.9	3.4	(3.3)	2.5	------	.9	------	------	------
21.3	1.5	6.9	(------)	------	3.1	3.8	------	10.7	2.2
.1	------	.1	(------)	------	------	.1	------	------	------
.2	------	(4)	(------)	------	------	(4)	------	------	.2
14.2	8.0	.6	(------)	------	------	.6	------	5.0	.6.
13.3	11.0	1.2	(------)	------	(4)	1.2	------	.4	.7
.4	------	.4	(------)	------	(4)	.4	------	------	------
2.9	2.9	------	(------)	------	------	------	------	------	------
62.1	.7	------	(------)	------	------	------	------	------	61.4
509.6	------	297.7	(229.9)	203.0	43.5	42.8	8.4	131.8	[7] 80.1
8.5	------	8.5	(10.7)	8.1	------	.4	------	------	------
(4)	------	(4)	(------)	------	------	(4)	------	------	------
41.7	------	41.7	[2](27.0)	21.9	3.5	7.9	8.4	------	------
5.6	------	5.6	(------)	------	2.9	2.7	------	------	------
86.6	------	86.4	[2](91.2)	82.1	.8	3.5	------	------	.2
123.8	------	.9	(------)	------	------	.9	------	122.9	------
78.1	------	78.1	(74.0)	66.6	1.4	10.1	------	------	------
.5	------	.5	(------)	------	------	.5	------	------	.8
2.2	------	1.4	(------)	------	------	1.4	------	------	------
90.9	------	9.8	(------)	------	------	9.8	------	3.9	77.2
6.4	------	.1	(------)	------	------	.1	------	5.0	1.3
64.4	------	64.4	(27.0)	24.3	34.8	5.3	------	------	------
.7	------	------	(------)	------	------	------	------	------	.7
264.9	------	231.7	(62.5)	53.4	136.8	37.3	4.2	19.2	[9] 14.0
77.8	------	77.8	(------)	------	63.8	14.0	------	------	------
1.5	------	1.5	(------)	------	.6	.9	------	------	------
.5	------	(4)	(------)	------	------	(4)	------	------	.5
(4)	------	(4)	(------)	------	------	(4)	------	------	------
.1	------	.1	(------)	------	------	.1	------	------	------
.2	------	------	(------)	------	------	------	------	..2	------
37.2	------	37.2	(30.6)	27.5	6.3	3.4	------	------	------
.3	------	.3	(------)	------	------	.3	------	------	------
5.2	------	3.)	(.9)	.7	------	.9	1.4	------	2.2

TABLE II—*Foreign aid, fisca*

Region and country	Grand total 100 countries and territories	Total military	ECONOMIC				
				AID programs			
			Total economic	AID total	Development grants/program social progress	Development loans	Supporting assistance and other
Africa—Con.							
Gabon	1.2	------	1.2	.7	.7	------	------
Ghana	3.0	.1	2.9	1.7	1.7	------	------
Guinea	16.0	------	16.0	12.1	3.7	2.4	6.0
Ivory Coast	7.9	.1	7.8	2.5	.8	1.7	------
Kenya	5.7	------	5.7	4.9	2.7	2.2	------
Liberia	50.8	2.1	48.7	39.9	8.6	31.3	------
Libya	12.5	1.1	11.4	10.4	1.4	------	9.0
Malagasy Republic	1.0	------	1.0	.5	.5	------	------
Mali, Republic of	4.6	.7	3.9	3.9	1.2	2.1	.7
Mauritania	.2	------	.2	.1	.1	------	(4).
Morocco	75.0	(3)	75.0	21.6	1.1	------	20.5
Niger	1.4	(4)	1.4	1.2	.7	.5	------
Nigeria	36.6	.2	36.4	24.1	12.0	12.1	------
Rhodesia and Nyasaland	2.2	------	2.2	1.8	1.8	------	------
Rwanda	(4)	------	(4)	------	------	------	------
Senegal	5.2	1.5	3.7	2.2	2.2	------	------
Sierra Leone	3.9	------	3.9	2.5	2.5	------	------
Somali Republic	9.2	------	9.2	7.8	4.2	3.6	------
Sudan	11.0	------	11.0	6.5	2.7	3.8	------
Tanganyika	12.5	------	12.5	8.9	2.0	6.9	------
Togo	1.3	------	1.3	.8	.8	------	------
Tunisia	71.9	(3)	71.9	32.3	2.2	23.3	6.8
Uganda	7.0	------	7.0	6.9	2.5	4.4	------
Upper Volta	1.0	(4)	1.0	.5	.5	------	------
Zanzibar	(4)	------	(4)	------	------	------	------
Other British territories	.1	------	.1	------	------	------	------
Regional	22.0	12.3	9.7	9.7	9.4	------	.3
Europe	899.1	476.4	422.7	2.9	2.9	------	------
Austria	31.4	------	31.4	------	------	------	------
Belgium-Luxembourg	28.1	28.1	------	------	------	------	------
Denmark	24.0	24.0	------	------	------	------	------
France	30.6	30.5	.1	------	------	------	------
Germany (Federal Republic)	.5	.3	.2	------	------	------	------
Iceland	1.4	------	1.4	------	------	------	------
Italy (including Trieste)	300.7	72.4	228.3	------	------	------	------
Netherlands	16.4	16.3	.1	------	------	------	------
Norway	38.7	38.7	------	------	------	------	------

Footnotes at end of table.

[In millions of dollars]

ear 1963 (preliminary report).

ASSISTANCE

		Other economic assistance							
		Food for peace—Public Law 480						Export-Import Bank long-term loans	Other economic programs
Total	Social progress trust fund	Total	Title I		Title II	Title III	Title IV		
			Total sales agreements	Planned for country use					
.5		(4)	(------)			(4)			.5
1.2		.6				.6			.6
3.9		3.6	[2] (4.7)	3.6				4.7	.3
5.3		(4)				(4)			.6
.8		.8			.6	.2			
8.8		3.0				.2	2.8	4.5	1.3
1.0									1.0
.5		.5				.5			
.1		.1	(------)		.1	(4)			
53.4		52.6	(7.7)	5.8	35.3	11.5			.8
.2									.2
12.3		.3				.3		9.5	2.5
.4		(4)				(4)			.4
(4)		(4)				(4)			
1.5		.6				.6		.3	.6
1.4		.5				.5			.9
1.4		1.2			1.2	(4)			.
4.5		4.5	(6.0)	4.5					
3.6		3.3			3.0	.3			.3
.5		.2				.2			.3
39.6		39.0	(12.6)	11.3	25.7	2.0			.6
.1		.1				.1			
.5		.5				.5			
(4)		(4)				(4)			
.1		.1	(------)			.1			(4)
(4)			(------)						
419.8		154.8	(145.8)	84.3	4.0	50.3	16.2	265.0	
31.4			(------)					31.4	
			(------)						
			(------)						
.1		.1	(------)			0			
.2		.2	(------)			.2			
1.4		1.4	(1.9)	1.4					
228.9		14.4	(------)		4.0	10.4		213.9	
.1		.1				.1			

TABLE II—*Foreign aid, fisca*

Region and country	Grand total 100 countries and territories	Total military	ECONOMIC				
			Total economic	AID programs			
				AID total	Development grants/ program social progress	Development loans	Supporting assistance and other
Europe—Continued							
Poland	10.8	--------	10.8	2.8	[10] 2.8	-----------	--------
Portugal	18.9	11.2	7.7	--------	-----------	-----------	--------
Spain	61.0	31.8	29.2	--------	-----------	-----------	--------
United Kingdom	11.2	11.2	--------	--------	-----------	-----------	--------
Yugoslavia	113.5	--------	113.5	.1	.1	-----------	--------
Regional	211.9	211.9	--------	--------	-----------	-----------	--------
Nonregional	459.9	106.1	363.8	169.8	44.6	-----------	125.2

[1] Represents Peace Corps.
[2] Includes proration of multiyear agreements.
[3] Military data classified and included in regional totals.
[4] Less than $50,000.
[5] Represents $60,000,000 subscription to Inter-American Development Bank; $15,-200,000 for Peace Corps; and $2,400,000 for Rama Road.
[6] Excludes refinancings of $72,000,000.

[In millions of dollars]

ear 1963 (preliminary report).

ASSISTANCE

		Other economic assistance							
		Food for peace—Public Law 480							
Total	Social progress trust fund	Total	Title I		Title II	Title III	Title IV	Export-Import Bank long-term loans	Other economic programs
			Total sales agreements	Planned for country use					
8.0	--------	8.0	(51.6)	--------	--------	8.0	--------	--------	--------
7.7	--------	7.7	(-----)	--------	--------	7.7	--------	--------	--------
29.2	--------	9.5	(-----)	--------	--------	9.5	--------	19.7	--------
113.4	--------	113.4	(92.1)	82.9	--------	14.3	16.2	--------	--------
124.0	--------	47.4	(-----)	--------	--------	47.4	--------	--------	[11] 136.6

[7] Represents $73,000,000 war damage claims in the Philippines and $7,100,000 for the Peace Corps.
[8] Includes aid to Australia and New Zealand.
[9] Represents $13,000,000 for the Peace Corps; and $1,000,000 in Libya for special purpose funds.
[10] For Krakow Research Hospital.
[11] Includes $61,700,000 subscription to the International Development Association and $72,100,000 for U.N. bonds.

Index

217